C000161111

CAMPAIGN 286

CATALAUNIAN FIELDS AD 451

Rome's last great battle

SIMON MACDOWALL ILLUSTRATED BY PETER DENNIS
Series editor Marcus Cowper

First published in Great Britain in 2015 by Osprey Publishing,
PO Box 883, Oxford, OX1 9PL, UK
PO Box 3985, New York, NY 10185-3985, USA
E-mail: info@ospreypublishing.com

© 2015 Osprey Publishing Ltd
OSPREY PUBLISHING IS PART OF BLOOMSBURY PUBLISHING LTD.

All rights reserved. Apart from any fair dealing for the purpose of private study, research, criticism or review, as permitted under the Copyright, Designs and Patents Act, 1988, no part of this publication may be reproduced, stored in a retrieval system, or transmitted in any form or by any means, electronic, electrical, chemical, mechanical, optical, photocopying, recording or otherwise, without the prior written permission of the copyright owner. Enquiries should be addressed to the Publishers.

A CIP catalogue record for this book is available from the British Library.

ISBN: 978 1 4728 0743 4
PDF e-book ISBN: 978 1 4728 0744 1
e-Pub ISBN: 978 1 4728 0745 8

Editorial by Ilios Publishing Ltd, Oxford, UK (www.iliospublishing.com)
Index by Alison Worthington
Typeset in Myriad Pro and Sabon
Maps by Bounford.com
3D bird's-eye views by The Black Spot
Battlescene illustrations by Peter Dennis
Originated by PDQ Media, Bungay, UK
Printed in China through Worldprint Ltd.

17 18 19 10 9 8 7 6 5 4

ARTIST'S NOTE

Readers may care to note that the original paintings from which the colour plates in this book were prepared are available for private sale. The Publishers retain all reproduction copyright whatsoever. All enquiries should be addressed to:
Peter Dennis, Fieldhead, The Park, Mansfield, Notts, NG18 2AT, UK
Email: magie.h@ntlworld.com
The Publishers regret that they can enter into no correspondence upon this matter.

THE WOODLAND TRUST

Osprey Publishing are supporting the Woodland Trust, the UK's leading woodland conservation charity, by funding the dedication of trees.

DEDICATION

To Caroline, who tramped around the battlefield with me and saw things that I missed.

AUTHOR'S NOTE

In order to make things easy to follow I have used modern place names rather than ancient ones. Therefore it is Troyes rather than Augustobona Tricassium and Orléans instead of Aurelianum or Cenabum. I make an exception where the ancient name is well known, such as Constantinople rather than modern Istanbul.

There are many spelling variations of barbarian names, no doubt because Roman writers used an approximation of what they thought they had heard which have since been anglicised over the years. Therefore the King of the Visigoths is variously known as Theodoric, Theodorid, Theodorich, or Thiudareiks. As with place names I have tried to use those in most common modern usage.

Unless specified otherwise, all photographs are from the author's collection.

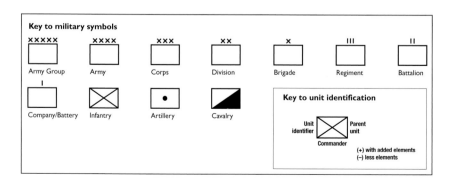

Key to military symbols

Army Group	Army	Corps	Division	Brigade	Regiment	Battalion
×××××	××××	×××	××	×	III	II

Company/Battery	Infantry	Artillery	Cavalry
I		•	

Key to unit identification

Unit identifier — Parent unit
Commander
(+) with added elements
(–) less elements

CONTENTS

ORIGINS OF THE CAMPAIGN

INTRODUCTION

On 20 June AD 451 a formidable invasion of Huns and Germans was defeated by an alliance of Romans, Alans, Goths and other Germans in a battle that took place on the plains of Champagne in France, known then as the Catalaunian Fields. The battle (more commonly and erroneously known as the Battle of Châlons) arguably changed the course of European history. It was included in Sir Edward Creasy's *The Fifteen Decisive Battles of the World* (1851) and, as Sir Edward Gibbon so eloquently put it, 'All the nations from the Volga to the Atlantic' took part.

For such an important battle, very little is known about it for certain. There is virtually no hard archaeological evidence and contemporary literary sources are patchy. The main primary description of the battle comes from Jordanes who, as a Gothic propagandist, glorified the Gothic actions in the battle (on both sides) and virtually ignored the parts played by other nationalities. The contemporary Greek historian Priscus actually met Attila but only fragments of his histories survive. These along with brief passages from the 5th-century Gallo-Roman aristocrat Sidonius Apollinaris, supplemented by the lives of early Christian saints, Gregory of Tours and various chroniclers are all we have to go on. Therefore, any reconstruction of the battle is a difficult task and must at times fall back on conjecture.

The Catalaunian Fields encompass the general area of modern Champagne between Châlons-en-Champagne and Troyes. We do not know for certain where the battle took place but one ancient source places it on the Campus Mauriacus, 7km from Troyes and 80km south of Châlons-en-Champagne. We know the nations involved but not their exact proportion or numbers; nor do we know much about what actually happened on the battlefield beyond the few tantalising snippets Jordanes has left us. That said, by pulling together the little bits of hard evidence combined with a detailed analysis of the possible battlefield sites, we can make some sense of what happened on that mid-summer day when the fate of Western Europe was decided.

This impressive 3rd-century hoard of Roman coins, now at the Musée Saint-Loup, was found near Troyes and was probably hidden by a wealthy Roman as he fled an invading army.

THE HUNS AND GOTHS

The Huns exploded into the Roman world in the mid-4th century. Their origin has been debated by historians over the centuries. Little is really known for certain about their early history other than the fact that they emerged from the Eurasian steppes and drove the Alans and Germans westward to seek refuge in the Roman Empire.

The Huns, as Ammianus Marcellinus, a 4th-century Roman officer, described, 'were the original cause of all the destruction and various calamities which the fury of Mars roused up, throwing everything into confusion by his usual ruinous violence … This active and indomitable race, being excited by an unrestrainable desire of plundering the possessions of others, went on ravaging and slaughtering all the nations in their neighbourhood till they reached the Alans'. Ammianus goes on to say how the Huns conquered the Alans and then kept pushing westwards. They defeated the Goths and sent thousands of refugees across the Danube to seek safety inside Roman territory.

The calamitous defeat of the Romans at the hands of the Goths is described in my previous Osprey Campaign book *Adrianople AD 378*. The descendants of the Gothic victors at Adrianople sacked Rome in 410 and in 418 were given land to settle in south-western France in exchange for waging war on the Vandals and Suebi who had occupied much of Spain. By 451 this branch of Goths had established a kingdom based around modern Toulouse. They were now often called 'Visigoths' to distinguish them from the eastern Goths (Ostrogoths) who remained beyond the Roman frontier and were under Hun dominion.

After subjugating the other barbarian tribes beyond the Danube, the Huns settled down on the Hungarian plain. They provided troops to support the West Romans while raiding the East and exacting extortionate tributes from Constantinople. By the mid-5th century the Hun empire, centred on modern Hungary, stretched back onto the eastern steppes and forward to the Rhine. They had subjugated or absorbed the Germanic, Sarmatian and Slavic populations of the region and were having a major impact on Roman politics and military capability. Not least of this was their value as allies and mercenaries in the West Roman army under the command of Flavius Aetius.

In 433 Aetius' friend and ally Rua, King of the Huns, died. He was succeeded by his nephews Bleda and Attila. When Attila murdered his brother and ruled alone, things began to change for the Romans. He prohibited Huns from serving Rome, which must have been a great blow to Aetius as they had formed the backbone of his armies for the past 20 years. In two campaigns against the Eastern Empire (441–42 and 447) the Huns devastated the Balkans and exacted an enormous tribute from Constantinople. By 448 the Eastern Empire was paying the Huns 6,000 pounds of gold per annum and had agreed to abandon much of the lower

The soldiers on the base of the Obelisk of Theodosius in the Hippodrome of Constantinople are probably depictions of late 4th-century Goths in Roman service. Their long hair, neck torques and lack of beards set them apart from the short-haired, bearded Romans. Interesting details include the fact that the bosses are off-centre and that the bottom of the shields seem to taper slightly. This may indicate a very early prototype of a 'kite shield' suitable for mounted action.

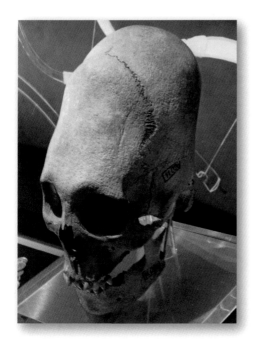

This female Hun skull has been artificially deformed by binding the head when a child. The Huns, Alans and many of the German tribes that fought for Attila followed this practice. It may have indicated high social status. (Hungarian National Museum)

Danube frontier as a buffer wasteland. Callinicus, who lived in Thrace at the time and would have experienced the Hun invasion first hand, describes the horror in his *Life of Saint Hypatius*: 'The barbarian nation of the Huns … became so great that more than a hundred cities were captured and Constantinople almost came into danger and most men fled from it … And there were so many murders and blood-lettings that the dead could not be numbered. Ay, for they took captive the churches and monasteries and slew the monks and maidens in great numbers.'

With the East Roman frontier laid to waste and her cities looted, Attila began to look elsewhere for a new source of wealth and prestige. His eyes turned to the West.

ROMAN GAUL

The Roman Empire had been divided into two halves since the 3rd century. By the 5th century, the Eastern Empire, ruled from Constantinople (modern Istanbul) and the Western Empire, ruled from Ravenna (Rome having been long abandoned as capital), were two often competing entities. Although both halves of the empire saw themselves as Roman and superior to the Hun and German barbarians, they tended to look to their own preservation first. Neither would hesitate from shifting a barbarian threat to the other half of the empire or even encouraging it if such action might preserve their own territorial integrity.

By the mid-5th century, Gaul (modern France and Belgium) was in a state of continuous turmoil. The frontiers had broken down: Vandals, Suebi, Alans, Franks, Alamanni, Visigoths and Burgundians had either overrun the country, seized parts of it for themselves, or had been given land to settle in return for military service in the Roman army. The native Gallo-Romans, harshly treated and taxed to the limit, had either fled to the protection of the great landowners – entering into voluntary serfdom – or had risen in revolt.

A Frankish warrior buried with his weapons, including *francisca*, spear and sword. Franks fought in both Aetius' and Attila's armies. This skeleton now resides at the Musée des Temps Barbares.

For more than 20 years Aetius was constantly on campaign in Gaul, fighting against the Bacaudae, Franks, Burgundians and Visigoths in order to keep Gaul secure.

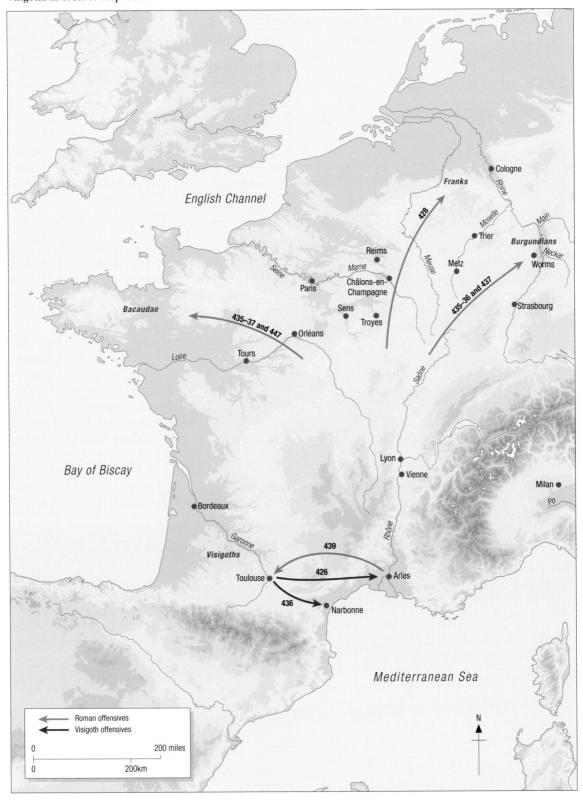

English Channel

Franks

Cologne

428

Trier

Moselle

Burgundians

Worms

Neckar

Metz

Reims

Marne

Châlons-en-
Champagne

Meuse

Strasbourg

Paris

Sens

Seine

Troyes

435–36 and 437

Bacaudae

435–37 and 447

Orléans

Loire

Tours

Saône

Bay of Biscay

Lyon

Vienne

Milan

Po

Bordeaux

Garonne

Visigoths

439

Rhône

Toulouse

426

Arles

436

Narbonne

Mediterranean Sea

N

→ Roman offensives
→ Visigoth offensives

0   200 miles
0   200km

7

In the midst of this confusion, the patrician Flavius Aetius took power with the backing of the Huns, with whom he had been a hostage as a child. In the 420s, with a formidable contingent of Hun mercenaries at his back, Aetius built up a power base in Gaul. He waged successful campaigns against the Franks and Visigoths and by 433 had defeated his main rival Count Boniface to become *Comes et Magister Utriusque Militiae* of the Western Empire – holding supreme military power.

Apart from dealing with the intrigues of the Roman court, the preservation of Roman Gaul was the keystone of Aetius' policy. At this time the Visigoths were expanding their power in the south-west; the Franks and Burgundians had spilled over the Rhine frontier and there had been serious peasant uprisings. An outlaw haven was established in Armorica (modern Brittany) by the Bacaudae. These were a collection of escaped slaves, peasants, army deserters and anyone wishing to escape the crushing burden of taxes. Under their leader Tibatto they had even begun minting their own coins and resisted any attempts by the imperial authorities to bring them back under control.

Aetius relied almost exclusively on the Huns to provide the troops he needed to subdue Gaul. Sidonius Apollinaris tells the tale of Avitus, the former *magister militum* (master of soldiers) defending his estates from pillaging Huns in the army of Litorius, Aetius' subordinate fighting the Goths in the 430s:

> Thus [Avitus] spoke and bounded forth into the midst of the plain; and the barbarous foe likewise came. When first they approached, breast to breast and face to face, the one shook with anger, the other with fear. Now the general throng stands in suspense, with prayers on this side or that, and as blow follows blow they hang in the issue. But when the first bout, the second, the third have been fought, lo! the upraised spear comes and pierces the man of blood [the Hun]; his breast was transfixed and his corselet twice split, giving way even where it covered the back and as the blood came throbbing through the two gaps the separate wounds took away the life that each of them might claim.

A Spanish re-enactor equipped as a 5th-century Roman infantryman. Such men would have formed the backbone of Aetius' native Roman forces. (Javier Gómez Valero)

The image of a former Roman general fighting a duel against a Hun in Roman service perfectly captures the confused loyalties of 5th-century Gaul. Many Romans had become enemies of the state by joining the Bacaudae to escape the heavy hand of taxation. Roman armies were made up of Huns or Alans while the Goths and Franks were settling down as overlords of south-western and northern Gaul respectively.

Over the 430s, with the Huns as his allies, Aetius checked the advances of the Franks, relieved the Visigoth siege of Arles and recovered Narbonne from them at a price of acknowledging their independence from Roman rule. In 437 he broke the power of the Burgundians and two years later he captured Tibatto and temporarily suppressed the Bacaudae rebellion. To help stop further advances by the Visigoths and to keep the Bacaudae of Armorica in check he set up a colony of Alans (a Sarmatian people) near Orléans. By the 440s, thanks to Aetius' efforts, Gaul was relatively stable despite continued Bacaudic uprisings. However, storm clouds were gathering in the East.

CAUSES OF WAR

The reasons why the Huns suddenly turned against the West Romans, with whom they had long been allies, are complex and convoluted. A wide variety of causes, some quite trivial, sparked off the conflict.

First of these was the accession of the new Eastern emperor Marcian in 450. He adopted a stronger policy towards the Huns than his predecessor Theodosius II. Marcian put a stop to the ruinous extortion extracted by the Huns in exchange for keeping the peace. Perhaps Attila's most obvious response would have been to renew war against the Eastern Empire, but what would this have achieved? There was probably not a copper plate worth having anywhere in the Balkans that had not already been looted. Yet safe behind the walls of Constantinople the true riches of the East were beyond Attila's grasp. He could have sought to occupy land in the Balkans as the Goths had done in the previous century, but after so many decades of continuous warfare the land was probably not worth holding.

Gaul, on the other hand, was still in contention. The Visigoths under Theodoric had carved out a kingdom in the south-west, based around modern Toulouse. The Franks had land along the lower Rhine frontier, the Alamanni were spilling over the upper Rhine and the Burgundians had been given land in what we now call Burgundy. Alans had been settled near Orléans, a band of Saxons had established itself nearby on the Loire, British refugees were moving into Brittany to join the Bacaudae and yet the Huns, who had been such faithful allies of the West Romans, still had no land within the empire to show for their loyalty. From Attila's point of view a campaign in Gaul in which he might supplant one or another of the various petty rival kingdoms surely seemed a more profitable enterprise than once again descending on the Balkans.

A possible claim to a legitimate holding for Attila within the Western Empire came from a rather unlikely source. Justa Grata Honoria, the sister of the Western emperor Valentinian III, became involved in a love scandal at court. Her lover, Eugenius, was executed and Honoria was set to be married off to a rather dull Roman senator to keep her from causing more trouble. In 450 Honoria appealed to Attila for help as her champion, sending him her ring as a token. Attila took this as a promise of marriage and demanded half

The massive walls of Constantinople kept the East Roman capital safe from several Hun incursions.

of the Western Empire as a dowry. In moving against the West, he could do so not simply as an invader but as someone claiming his right as the emperor's future brother-in-law.

Meanwhile the Franks, who had spilled over the lower Rhine frontier, were fighting amongst themselves over leadership following the death of Chlodio at the end of the 440s. According to Priscus, Chlodio's eldest son sought assistance from Attila to claim his inheritance. A younger brother sought help from Aetius who had adopted him as a son during an earlier Frankish embassy to Rome.

If these were not enough reasons to consider an invasion of Gaul, the Vandals in Africa were encouraging the Huns to move against the Visigoths. According to Jordanes:

> When Gaiseric, king of the Vandals, learned that Attila's mind was bent on the devastation of the world, he incited him by many gifts to make war on the Visigoths, for he was afraid that Theodoric, king of the Visigoths, would avenge the injury done to his daughter. She had been joined in wedlock with Huneric, Gaiseric's son, and at first was happy in this union. But afterwards he was cruel even to his own children, and because of the mere suspicion that she was attempting to poison him, he cut off her nose and mutilated her ears. He sent her back to her father in Gaul thus despoiled of her natural charms. So the wretched girl presented a pitiable aspect ever after, and the cruelty which would stir even strangers still more surely incited her father to vengeance.

Concerned that Theodoric would lead the Visigoths against him to avenge his daughter's honour, Gaiseric sought an alliance with the Huns. He probably hoped that if the Huns threatened the Visigoths, the latter would be in no position to wage war on him. From Attila's point of view he possibly saw a great opportunity to supplant the Visigoths in southern Gaul while establishing a client kingdom of Franks in the north by supporting the eldest of Chlodio's sons. With Honoria as his wife he could have taken over the territories occupied by Aetius' enemies and continued the previous Hun policy of supporting the West with the added benefit of land within the empire and a direct connection to the throne. Priscus comments:

> Attila was of two minds and at a loss which he should attack first [the East or West Roman empires]. But it seemed better to him to enter on the greater war and to march against the West, since his fight there would not be only against the Italians but also against the Goths and Franks. Against the Italians so as to seize Honoria along with her money, and against the Goths in order to earn the gratitude of Gaiseric, the Vandal King. Attila's excuse for war against the Franks was the death of their king and the disagreement of his children over the rule.

In order to keep the loyalty of his many followers and subject tribes Attila needed to distribute wealth and honour. With an end to the tribute from the Eastern Empire he could not afford to accept the status quo. He had to go to war and the most profitable target was Gaul.

With all this happening, what then was Aetius thinking? When Attila made his move, it seems as though Aetius was caught off guard. Quite

By the mid-5th century AD a number of barbarian tribes had been granted land to settle inside the Roman Empire in return for military service. Meanwhile the Huns under Attila ruled over a huge empire stretching from the Rhine to beyond the Black Sea.

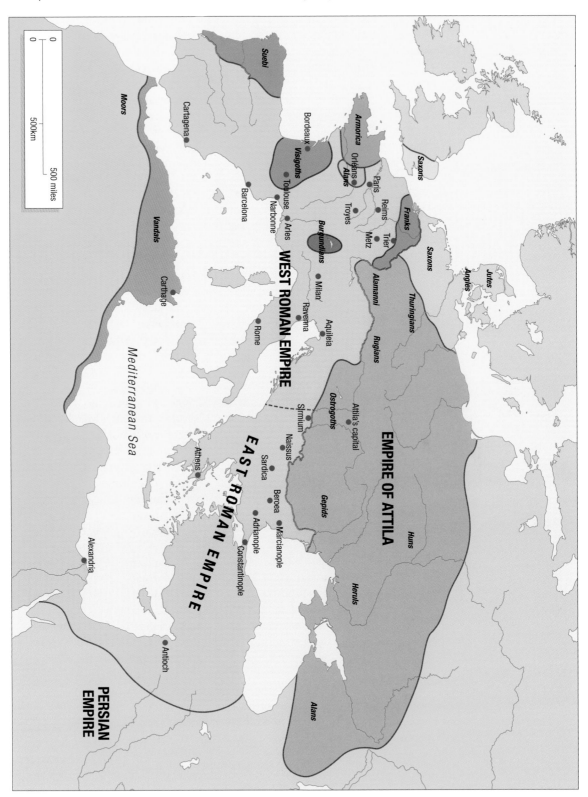

possibly he had assumed that if the Eastern Empire decided to end the tribute then the Huns would naturally have renewed war against them. Only two years before Attila's invasion, Priscus records meeting 'Constantius, an Italian whom Aetius had sent to Attila to be that monarch's private secretary.' This shows that Aetius still saw Attila as a potential friend and ally.

Attila probably assumed that the West Romans would prefer his presence in Gaul to that of the Visigoths, who had long been Roman enemies. Similarly Aetius likely assumed that Huns, who had always been his friends and allies, would never turn against him. Both assumptions proved to be untrue.

When Attila made his move in the spring of 451, Aetius was in Italy. Gaul was more or less undefended. Whatever remained of the Roman forces in Gaul had been run down or ignored for a generation. For more than 20 years Aetius had relied on Huns and Alans to secure his authority against the Visigoths, Franks, Burgundians and Bacaudae. With the Huns suddenly his opponents, Aetius had to turn to the Visigoths for support.

If Attila had calculated that the West Romans would rather have had Huns settled in Gaul in place of the Visigoths, why then did Aetius join up with his former enemies to oppose his former Hun allies?

There is no simple answer to this question but a sudden attack against his power base probably left Aetius no choice. Attila did not approach him first with a proposition to take on the Visigoths in the name of Rome. Rather he had demanded an impossible dowry for Honoria's hand in marriage. If Aetius had simply stood aside and allowed Attila to take what he wanted, his own power would have been fatally weakened. Gaul was in effect Aetius' kingdom and he had to defend it even if he may have secretly wished to have the Huns supporting him rather than the Visigoths.

The problem for Aetius was that he had very few troops. While Attila could call on all the Huns and their many subject German tribes for support, Aetius had nothing to match him. Until now the mainstay of all Aetius' armies had been his Hun allies. With the Huns now his enemies and the Gallo-Roman garrisons run down, ignored, or gone over to the Bacaudae, Aetius had no choice but to turn to the Visigoths for help.

Aetius called on Avitus to help him convince the Visigoths that they would be better off by throwing their lot in with the Romans rather than simply defending their territory:

> 'Your influence alone is a barrier-wall to the Gothic people; ever hostile to us, they grant peace to you. Go, display the victorious eagles; bring it to pass, O noble hero, that the Huns, whose flight afore time shook us, shall by a second defeat be made to do me service.' Thus [Aetius] spoke and Avitus consenting changed his prayer into hope. Straightway he rouses up the Gothic fury that was his willing slave. Rushing to enrol their names the skin-clad warriors began to march behind the Roman trumpets. (Sidonius Apollinaris)

The stage was set. Attila, supported by his subject German tribes, marched east towards the Rhine in the spring of 451. Aetius, having secured an alliance with the Visigoths, moved north to stop him.

CHRONOLOGY

370s

The Huns move west defeating the Alans and the Goths.

376

Fleeing the Huns, some Goths seek refuge in the East Roman Empire.

378
9 August

The East Roman army is crushed by the Goths at the Battle of Adrianople.

382

The Goths are given land to settle in Moesia in return for providing troops for the East Roman army.

395

The Goths, led by Alaric, rise in revolt after the death of the Emperor Theodosius I.

406–07

Vandals, Alans and Suebi cross the Rhine in mid-winter. They overrun Gaul and eventually move into Spain.

408

Theodosius II becomes East Roman Emperor.

410

Alaric's Goths sack Rome.

418

The Goths are granted land in south-western France, centred on Toulouse, in exchange for military action against the Vandals, Alans and Suebi in Spain and the Bacaudae in Armorica. Theodoric becomes king.

422

Hun raids into Thrace are bought off with a tribute from the Eastern Empire.

423

Death of the Western emperor Honorius.

423–25

Joannes usurps the West Roman throne.

424

Joannes sends Aetius on a mission to the Huns to gain military support.

425

Joannes is overthrown by an East Roman army led by Aspar. The infant Valentinian III becomes Emperor of the West with his mother Galla Placidia as regent. Three days after Joannes' death Aetius returns with an army of Huns. Galla Placidia buys him off by appointing him as the regional commander of Gaul (*magister militum per Gallias*).

426–30

Aetius campaigns against the Visigoths and Franks in Gaul.

429

Vandals under Gaiseric cross from Spain to Africa.

430

Aetius assassinates Felix, the *magister militum*.

432

Boniface defeats Aetius at the Battle of Rimini but is mortally wounded. Aetius seeks refuge with the Huns.

433

Rua, King of the Huns, dies and is succeeded by Attila and Bleda. Aetius, returning with Hun support, is given supreme military power in the West as *Comes et Magister Utriusque Militiae*.

435

Treaty of Margus with the Eastern Empire gives the Huns trading rights and an annual tribute of 700 pounds of gold.

435–37

Aetius campaigns against the Bacaudae of Armorica and captures their leader Tibatto, who later escapes.

436

Aetius attacks and defeats the Burgundians at Worms.

437

Hun allies in Aetius' service destroy the Burgundian kingdom on the Rhine.

435–39

Renewed conflict between the Romans and Visigoths ends in stalemate.

439

Carthage falls to the Vandals.

440

An East Roman expedition sails to recapture Carthage. The Persians invade Roman Armenia. Taking advantage of this, the Huns raid across the Danube.

441–43

The East Roman expedition to Carthage is recalled having accomplished nothing. The Huns devastate the Balkans, capturing many cities and defeating two East Roman armies. Constantinople is only saved by the strength of its walls.

442

The Vandal Huneric mutilates his wife, the daughter of King Theodoric, creating a feud between the Vandals and Visigoths.

443

The Eastern Emperor Theodosius II sues for peace and agrees to increase the annual tribute to 6,000 pounds of gold in exchange for an uneasy truce.

441–43

West Roman campaign against the Bacaudae in Spain.

442

A group of Alans led by Goar is given land near Orléans to keep the Bacaudae of Armorica in check. Goar is later succeeded by Sangiban.

443

The surviving Burgundians are resettled in Savoy in exchange for military service in the West Roman army.

445

Bleda dies, probably murdered by Attila, who now becomes sole ruler of the Huns.

447

Attila invades the East Roman Empire and defeats Arnegisclus at the Battle of Utus River. The Huns once again lay waste to the Balkans. The walls of Constantinople are seriously damaged by an earthquake and the city is ravaged by plague. The Consul Constantius rebuilds the walls and a hasty defence is organised by Zeno, commanding Isaurian auxiliaries.

447–49

Renewed Bacaudic uprisings in Armorica and Spain.

448

A new peace treaty is concluded between the Huns and the Eastern Empire in which the Romans agree to abandon much of the Danube frontier.

450

Honoria appeals to Attila for support. Theodosius II dies and is succeeded by Marcian as Emperor of the East.

451

Attila invades Gaul and is defeated by Aetius and Theodoric at Catalaunian Fields. Thorismund succeeds his father as King of the Visigoths.

452

Attila invades Italy.

453

Death of Attila. Theodoric II kills his elder brother Thorismund to take the Visigoth throne.

454

The Huns are defeated at the Battle of Nedao by a coalition of Germans led by Ardaric, King of the Gepids. Aetius is murdered by Valentinian III.

455

Valentinian is murdered by Aetius' former guards. The Vandals sack Rome.

475

Orestes, Attila's former secretary, makes his son Romulus West Roman Emperor.

476

Odoacer overthrows Romulus and becomes King of Italy.

By the mid-5th century, the Roman defences of the Rhine frontier had been largely replaced by settlements of Franks, Burgundians and Alamanni who held land in exchange for military service. This reconstructed village at the Musée des Temps Barbares would have been typical of such settlements.

OPPOSING COMMANDERS

THE ROMANS AND THEIR ALLIES

Flavius Aetius (391–454) spent his childhood as a hostage of both the Goths and the Huns. He developed a close relationship with the latter and relied on them for support in a series of civil wars from which he emerged as the most powerful man in the Western Empire. He set himself the task of establishing a power base in Gaul, defending it from internal and external threats at the expense of all other regions of the Western Empire.

An ivory diptych which possibly shows Aetius. If so this is the only representation of the 'last of the Romans'. (Musée du Berry, Bourges)

Aetius was born at Silistra in Moesia on the lower Danube. Aetius' mother was a wealthy Italian noblewoman and his father, Gaudentius, a prominent general of barbarian origin who rose to the rank of master of cavalry (*magister equitum*).

A description of Aetius has survived. Although it is the work of a panegyrist that exaggerates Aetius' good points, it may give us some idea of what the man was like:

The graceful figure of Aetius was not above the middle stature … he excelled in the martial exercises of managing a horse, drawing a bow and darting the javelin. He could patiently endure the want of food or sleep and his mind and body were alike capable of the most labourious efforts. He possessed the genuine courage that can despise not only dangers but injuries.

It is perhaps a comment on the changing nature of Roman warfare that the military qualities first mentioned are those of a horseman and archer. Clearly Aetius learned many of his skills as a warrior from the Huns.

When the Emperor Honorius died in 423, Aetius raised an army of Huns (allegedly and improbably 60,000 of them) to support the pretender Joannes. By the time Aetius arrived in Italy, Joannes had been deposed and the 7-year-old Valentinian was on the throne with his mother Galla Placidia the power behind it. A general with an army of Huns at his back was still a force to be reckoned with, so Galla Placidia bought Aetius off with a command in Gaul and gold for his Hun followers.

With the support of the Huns, Aetius built up his power in Gaul. In 430 he assassinated Felix the master of soldiers (*magister militum*) and assumed his place. However Galla Placidia gave the position to Boniface the count of Africa (*comes africae*). When Aetius refused to give up the post, conflict broke out. Aetius lost the initial battle at Rimini in 432 and was forced to flee to the Huns. Boniface, however, was mortally wounded (or died of disease according to another source) and the following year Aetius returned with another Hun army at his back to assume supreme power.

For the next 18 years Aetius concentrated on defending Gaul, waging successful campaigns against the Franks, Visigoths, Burgundians and Bacaudae. To stop further advances by the Visigoths and to pacify the Bacaudae of Armorica he established a military colony of Alans around Orléans. He used the Huns to ruthlessly break the power of the Burgundians on the middle Rhine and resettled the survivors in Savoy. The destruction of the Burgundian kingdom of Worms by the Huns became the subject of heroic legends that formed the base of the *Nibelungenlied* and Wagner's *Ring Cycle*. This event is recounted in the chronicle of Prosper: 'Aetius crushed in battle Gundicharius, the king of the Burgundians living within Gaul, and gave him the peace he asked for. But Gundicharius did not enjoy that peace for long, since the Huns utterly destroyed him and his people.'

Aetius made no attempt to recover Britain, Spain or Africa. He treated Gaul almost as his personal fiefdom and spent all his efforts to keep it secure. When Attila invaded Gaul in 451, Aetius was faced with a nearly insurmountable problem. The men who had been the backbone of his armies for over 20 years were now his opponents. If he lost Gaul, he would lose everything, and he had to turn to his former enemies for help. The coalition that he was able to cobble together to stop Attila was very much a marriage of convenience. He had no desire to see the Visigoths or Franks become even more powerful but he had no choice except to seek their help. He would strive to ensure that once the battle was won, he would do what he could to prevent them from exploiting any victory. He had to stop Attila but he probably did not want Hun power to be completely broken. They provided a useful counter to the Visigoths and no doubt he hoped to be able to draw on their support again once Gaul was safe.

Probably Aetius cut a deal with the Bacaudae and recent British immigrants to Armorica, offering them freedom from imperial authority in exchange for their support. His campaigns against them in the 430s and 440s had taken a great deal of effort with little to show for it. Giving them independence was possibly little more than a recognition of the status quo.

Aetius' strategy, therefore, was to stop Attila but to ensure that in doing so he was still the most powerful warlord in Gaul. He would need to use allies to help him do this but he had no intention of letting them profit too much by their support.

This wood carving, from Monza Cathedral, is of the 4th-century general Stilicho. It is often erroneously said to depict Aetius.

THE DESTRUCTION OF THE BURGUNDIANS (PP. 18–19)

In the 430s Aetius relied almost exclusively on his Hun allies to secure his control of Gaul. They fought for him against the Visigoths, Franks, Bacaudae and most famously the Burgundians. This scene captures the moment when Huns in Roman service destroyed the Burgundian kingdom on the Rhine, near modern Worms – an event which became the subject of heroic legends that formed the base of the *Nibelungenlied* and Wagner's operatic *Ring Cycle*.

Weakened by his wounds, the Burgundian King Gundicharius **(1)** is barely able to lift his sword to fend off a new attack by mounted Hun warriors. His retainers are rushing to his rescue but his life and his kingdom are doomed. The king is magnificently equipped in the height of Germanic style with mail, gilded spangenhelm and a fine pattern welded sword. Although lacking mail, Gundicharius' retainers **(2)** are also well equipped. Their highly decorated, loose over-tunics are typical of the Western Germanic warrior elite.

Although famously horse archers, the Huns were perfectly happy closing to hand-to-hand combat. This Hun **(3)** has put his bow aside and is galloping in for the kill with his spear. The high-fronted saddle and horse trappings are of Asiatic origin while his clothing is Roman. His lamellar armour also probably comes from the East rather than a Western armoury, but his helmet is Roman and has been personalised with the addition of a marmot tail.

Having access to Roman armouries this man **(4)** is almost entirely kitted out in Roman style and apart from his bow there is little to distinguish him from a regular Roman cavalryman. To aid rapid shooting he holds a number of arrows in his left hand against the front of his bow.

The dead Burgundian warrior **(5)** was unable to use his *francisca*, or throwing axe, before succumbing to the Hun arrows. His short sword, known as a seax or scramasax, lies on the ground beside him.

Flavius Placidius Valentinianus Augustus (419–55) – Valentinian III – became Western Roman emperor as a child. His mother Galla Placidia ran the empire as his regent until 437. By the time he had reached his majority, the affairs of state were well and truly in the hands of others, first his mother and then Aetius. He was an emperor in name only and although he was technically the ultimate power in the land, he had little opportunity to exercise it. Valentinian must have resented Aetius' power and perhaps this is one reason why he gave Aetius such little support from Italy when the Huns invaded Gaul. When Attila invaded Italy in 452, Valentinian apparently sidelined Aetius. Two years later he killed Aetius with his own hands, only to be murdered in turn the following year by two of Aetius' personal retainers.

Flavius Maccilius Eparchius Avitus (c.385–456) was a Gallo-Roman aristocrat and son-in-law of Sidonius Apollinaris, whose writings are an important source for the goings on of the time. Avitus and his family had good relations with the Visigoths and it was primarily due to Avitus' influence that the Visigoths were persuaded to join an active alliance against Attila. He served as *magister militum* under Aetius in the 430s but apparently retired in the 440s. It is possible that he served on the field with Aetius and Theodoric in 451 but, as Sidonius Apollinaris does not mention this, it is more likely that he stayed home and sent one of his protégés instead. Four years after the battle Avitus was active again, filling the vacuum resulting from Aeitus' murder. He was proclaimed Western emperor by the Visigoths in 455 and reigned for three years.

It is doubtful that Avitus had his eye on the purple when he supported Aetius in 451. His strategy was to preserve his estates in southern Gaul and he saw the Visigoths as the key to this. Although a Roman, and briefly West Roman emperor, it is probably more realistic to see him as a trusted advisor to the Visigoths rather than a close ally of Aetius.

Flavius Marcianus Augustus (392–457) – Marcian – became East Roman emperor in 450. He was an Illyrian of humble origins, son of a soldier; he was a prominent soldier himself, and fought against the Persians, Vandals and Huns. On ascension he immediately adopted a more aggressive policy against the Huns. His predecessor, Theodosius II, had bought off the Huns with a huge tribute and Marcian put a stop to this. Rather than igniting a new war with the Huns the immediate effect was to cause Attila to look to the West as a new untapped source of wealth. Marcian's strategy was to revive the strength of the Eastern Empire even if this meant leaving the West to its fate.

This diptych, now in the Bibliothèque Nationale, Paris, is thought to show Felix, who was assassinated by Aetius in 430. (Sailko)

A silver dish in the Real Academia de la Historia, Madrid, shows the Emperor Theodosius I. His guardsmen, with their long hair, neck torques and clean-shaven faces, bear a close resemblance to those on the Theodosius Obelisk and are probably Goths. (Manuel de Corselas)

Theodoric I, King of the Visigoths (418–51), established a vibrant kingdom in south-western France based around modern Toulouse. He was an illegitimate son of Alaric and had been born within the Roman Empire. He was not, therefore, a barbarian invader but rather someone who strove to meld Roman and Gothic cultures while taking every opportunity to exploit Roman weakness to expand his own kingdom. For most of his reign he was in conflict with Aetius as he pushed the boundaries of the treaties he had concluded with the imperial authorities. Attila's invasion of Gaul threatened his position as much as that of Aetius. He might, however, have decided to remain at home and simply defend his territory but was persuaded to actively join the Roman cause through the influence of Avitus. The alliance he formed with Aetius was never going to survive the defeat of the Huns. Theodoric was killed in the Battle of the Catalaunian Fields.

Thorismund was Theodoric's eldest son. According to Jordanes, Theodoric 'sent home four of his sons, namely Friderich and Eurich, Retemer and Mimnerith, taking with him only the two elder sons, Thorismund and Theodoric, as partners of his toil.' Thorismund played a key role in the battle. He led an advance force that contested some high ground early in the engagement and then headed a decisive charge into the flank of the Huns and Ostrogoths, effectively winning the day. He was proclaimed king on the battlefield following his father's death.

There was no love lost between the sons of Theodoric I. When the battle was over, Thorismund hurried back to his capital at Toulouse to secure his crown against a possible coup by his younger brothers. As it was, Thorismund only reigned for two years before being murdered and supplanted by his younger brother Theodoric.

Theodoric II, Thorismund's younger brother, was also present at the battle but his actions are not recorded. Presumably he played a subordinate role, probably fighting alongside his father in the main Visigoth line. He became king of the Visigoths after murdering Thorismund in 453, ruling until 466, when he in turn was murdered by his younger brother Eurich.

Sidonius Apollinaris wrote a detailed description of Theodoric II after he became king:

> He is well set up, in height above the average man, but below the giant. His head is round, with curled hair retreating somewhat from brow to crown … The eyebrows are bushy and arched; when the lids droop, the lashes reach almost half-way down the cheeks. The upper ears are buried under overlying locks, after the fashion of his race … his barber is assiduous in eradicating the rich growth on the lower part of the face…
>
> Before daybreak he goes with a very small suite to attend the service of his priests. He prays with assiduity, but, if I may speak in confidence, one may

suspect more of habit than conviction in this piety. Administrative duties of the kingdom take up the rest of the morning. Armed nobles stand about the royal seat; the mass of guards in their garb of skins are admitted that they may be within call, but kept at the threshold for quiet's sake.

It is interesting to note the passage about Theodoric being clean-shaven. Despite popular images of bearded barbarians and clean-shaven Romans, contemporary depictions (coins and monuments) usually show Goths as clean-shaven and Romans with short beards.

Sangiban – the leader of the Alans – played a duplicitous game, but eventually came over to Aetius' side. As Attila advanced west, Sangiban was 'smitten with fear of what might come to pass, had promised to surrender to Attila, and to give into his keeping Aurelianum [Orléans], a city of Gaul wherein he dwelt' (Jordanes). Aetius and Theodoric got to Orléans first and, to continue Jordanes' narrative, 'kept watch over the suspected Sangiban, placing him with his tribe in the midst of their auxiliaries.'

It is unclear whether Sangiban was actively supporting Attila at the onset of the campaign or rather had decided to hand over Orléans because he could not have hoped to defend his lands against a much larger army. Either way, Sangiban's strategy was to try to end up on the winning side and therefore retain his lands in western France. According to Jordanes, Aetius deployed the Alans in the centre of the army in order to keep a close eye on them. Sangiban's fate after the battle is unknown.

Merovech (or Meroveus), the semi-legendary Frank who gave his name to the Merovingian dynasty, may have been the leader of the Franks who sided with Aetius. The case for this seems to have been made by French scholars in the early 18th century and was taken up by Sir Edward Gibbon. There are, however, no primary sources to back it up.

Very little is known about Merovech. According to Gregory of Tours: 'some say that Merovech, the father of Childeric, was descended from Chlodio.' The *Chronicle of Fredegar* relates a legend in which Merovech is conceived when Chlodio's wife goes swimming and meets a sea monster, 'the beast of Neptune which resembles a Quinotaur.'

Priscus writes: 'Attila's excuse for war against the Franks was the death of their king and the disagreement of his children over the rule, the elder who decided to bring Attila in as his ally, and the younger, Aetius. I saw this boy when he was at Rome on an embassy, a lad without down on his cheeks as yet and with fair hair so long that it poured down his shoulders. Aetius had made him his adopted son.'

Chlodio died just before Attila's invasion so Priscus' unnamed Frankish princes could have been his sons and one of them could have been Merovech. We will

The Hornhausen relief, now in the Landesmuseum für Vorgeschichte, Halle, is a rare depiction of a mounted Germanic warrior. Although from a later period, such men fought both for Aetius and Attila.

The ring of Childeric, King of the Franks, who may have been the son of the Frankish prince who supported Aetius at the Battle of Campus Mauriacus. (© Ashmolean Museum)

never know for certain. The strategy of the prince who led the Frankish contingent in Aetius' army was to secure undisputed leadership of the Franks by defeating his brother and then with Roman support consolidate his kingdom. Even if Merovech had not been at Aetius' side, his son Childeric, who became king around 458, would have become the undisputed leader of the Franks.

THE HUNS AND THEIR ALLIES

The rise to power of **Attila, King of the Huns** (434–53), is concisely documented by Jordanes:

> Now this Attila was the son of Mundiuch [or Mundzuk], and Mundiuch's brothers were Octar and Rua [or Rugila] who are said to have ruled before Attila, though not over quite so many tribes as he. After their death he succeeded to the throne of the Huns, together with his brother Bleda. In order that he might first be equal to the expedition he was preparing, he sought to increase his strength by murder. Thus he proceeded from the destruction of his own kindred to the menace of all others. But though he increased his power by this shameful means, yet by the balance of justice he received the hideous consequences of his own cruelty. Now when his brother Bleda, who ruled over a great part of the Huns, had been slain by his treachery, Attila united all the people under his own rule.

There are almost no contemporary depictions of Huns. This coin, however, is believed to depict a Hun ruler in the Far East who would have been a contemporary of Attila. The shape of his head shows the effect of skull deformation. (© British Museum)

For most of the early part of his reign, Attila maintained good relations with Aetius and the West while building up his power and prestige primarily at the expense of the Eastern Empire. He and Bleda succeeded Rua in 434, inheriting an empire centred on the Hungarian plain extending from the Danube to the Eurasian steppes. In that year the Huns concluded a successful treaty with the East Roman Empire in which they extracted an annual tribute, received trading rights and an agreement that the Romans would return all fugitives who sought refuge in imperial territory.

The Greek historian Priscus visited Attila's encampment in 448 on a diplomatic mission. He describes arriving 'at a large village, where Attila's house was said to be more splendid than his residences in other places. It was made of polished boards, and surrounded with a wooden enclosure, designed, not for protection, but for appearance'. Yet Attila seemed to have taken pains to portray himself as a man who shunned luxury:

> A luxurious meal, served on silver plate, had been made ready for us and the barbarian guests, but Attila ate nothing but meat on a wooden trencher. In everything else, too, he showed himself temperate; his cup was of wood, while to the guests were given goblets of gold and silver. His dress, too, was quite simple, affecting only to be clean. The sword he carried at his side, the latchets of his Scythian shoes, the bridle of his horse were not adorned, like those of the other Scythians, with gold or gems or anything costly. (Priscus)

Much of Priscus' account of his embassy to Attila survives, providing a fascinating insight into the world of the Huns. Priscus' physical description of Attila is preserved by Jordanes:

> He was haughty in his walk, rolling his eyes hither and thither, so that the power of his proud spirit appeared in the movement of his body. He was indeed a lover of war, yet restrained in action, mighty in counsel, gracious to suppliants and lenient to those who were once received into his protection. He was short of stature, with a broad chest and a large head; his eyes were small, his beard thin and sprinkled with grey; and he had a flat nose and a swarthy complexion, showing the evidences of his origin.

Ruling over a polyglot empire of subject and allied tribes, Attila's power rested on his ability to reward his followers with increasing amounts of wealth and glory. To this end he reopened hostilities with the Eastern Empire in 440. After laying waste to the Balkan frontier provinces, defeating several Roman armies and only being checked by the walls of Constantinople, he concluded yet another peace treaty which increased the tribute paid to him.

When the Emperor Theodosius II died in 450 and his successor Marcian refused to pay the tribute, Attila had two choices: go to war against the Eastern Empire again, or find another source of wealth. His decision to turn against the Western Empire was in part prompted by the knowledge that there was probably little more he could extract from the East. It must also have rankled that while the Visigoths, Vandals, Franks, Alans and Burgundians all had land within Roman territory and were able to enjoy all that Roman civilisation could offer, the Huns were excluded. Despite years of faithful service to the Western Empire and many successful campaigns against the East, the Huns were still kept beyond the frontiers.

Attila invaded Gaul with the intent of wresting significant concessions from the Western Empire. This may have included winning good land to settle within her borders and being accepted as pre-eminent amongst Rome's nominal allies. To this end he was probably going to war against the Visigoths and Franks as much or more than going to war against the Romans. For more than 20 years the Huns had propped up Aetius against the Visigoths, Franks, Burgundians, Bacaudae and rival Roman warlords. Was it too much

Throughout the 440s the Huns raided the Eastern Empire, defeated a Roman army at the Battle of Utus River and extracted a huge tribute from Constantinople.

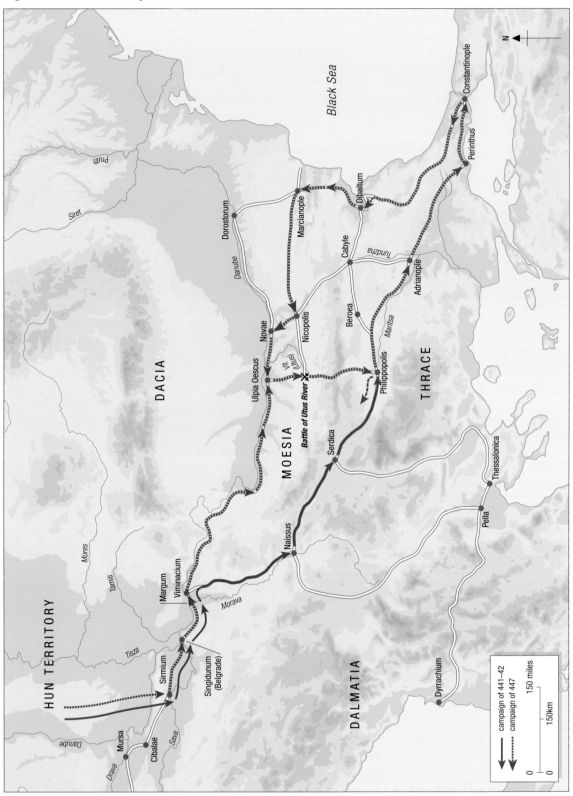

to expect that a show of strength would force the Western Empire to accept terms and give him land in Gaul at the expense of the other barbarian kingdoms?

With the benefit of hindsight we can see that Attila miscalculated. Yet how could he have foreseen the unlikely alliance between Aetius and his arch-enemies the Visigoths? When he crossed the Rhine in the spring of 451, Attila probably assumed that Aetius would have been forced to come to terms, possibly letting the Huns take over lands previously occupied by his enemies. The Romano-Visigoth alliance put paid to this and forced Attila to fight a battle he did not want to fight. He could not avoid the battle. To do so would have seriously weakened his authority and encouraged others to challenge him.

Other Hun commanders

We do not know anything of the other Hun leaders who may have held commands on the Catalaunian Fields. Three of Attila's sons, Ellac (the eldest), Dengizic (or Dintzic) and Ernac, vied for power after their father's death and may have been present at the battle. When Priscus visited Attila a couple of years earlier, he says that Onegesius was his principal lieutenant. Therefore Onegesius could have held a command in the battle, although it is just as likely that he was left behind to keep an eye on the home front.

From Priscus' description it seems as though Attila may have had a soft spot for his youngest son Ernac, while the elder brothers were cowed by their father:

> Onegesius sat on a chair on the right of Attila's couch, and beyond Onegesius sat two of Attila's sons; his eldest son sat, not near him but at the extreme end, with his eyes fixed on the ground in shy respect for his father … Attila, however, remained immovable and of unchanging countenance nor by word or act did he betray anything approaching a smile except at the entry of Ernac, his youngest son, whom he pulled by the cheek, and gazed on with a calm look of satisfaction.

Ardaric, King of the Gepids, commanded the prestigious right wing at the Catalaunian Fields. Ardaric was perhaps Attila's most trusted ally: 'The renowned king of the Gepids, Ardaric, was there also with a countless host, and because of his great loyalty to Attila, he shared his plans. For Attila, comparing them in his wisdom, prized him and Valamir, King of the Ostrogoths above all the other chieftains' (Jordanes).

The Gepids were an East Germanic tribe related to the Goths. When Attila died, Ardaric led a revolt against his sons, defeating the Huns at the Battle of Nedao in 454 and breaking their power forever. As a result some have assumed that Ardaric and the Gepids were not fully behind Attila in 451. Jordanes reinforces this idea in his description of the revolt:

This ring from the treasure of Pouan at the Musée Saint-Loup, Troyes, may have belonged to one of Attila's followers. Who Heva was remains a mystery.

> Ardaric, king of the Gepids … became enraged because so many nations were being treated like slaves of the basest condition, and was the first to rise against the sons of Attila. Good fortune attended him, and he effaced the disgrace of servitude that rested upon him. For by his revolt he freed not only his own tribe, but all the others who were equally oppressed.

In the 5th century loyalty was a very personal matter and not necessarily based on nationality or race. Ardaric could easily have been Attila's most trusted subject even though he was not a Hun. On Attila's death Ardaric would not have had any obligation to carry such loyalty over to his sons. Bickering over their inheritance and treating their allies with a high hand probably alienated Attila's sons from their subjects and does not necessarily mean that Ardaric felt the same way about the father. In all probability Ardaric and the Gepids fully supported Attila because they believed he would lead them to victory and bring them honour and a share of the spoils.

The Ostrogoth brothers **Valamir**, **Thiudimir** and **Vidimir** (there are other variations on the spelling) commanded Attila's left wing. Valamir was the senior but it seems as though the younger brothers had a degree of autonomy:

Valamir ascended the throne after his parents, though the Huns as yet held the power over the Goths

This gilded helmet from Deurne in the Netherlands is inscribed as originally belonging to a Roman cavalryman of the Equites Stablesiani. (Michiel)

in general as among other nations. It was pleasant to behold the concord of these three brothers; for the admirable Thiudimir served as a soldier for the empire of his brother Valamir, and Valamir bade honours be given him, while Vidimir was eager to serve them both. Thus regarding one another with common affection, not one was wholly deprived of the kingdom which two of them held in mutual peace.

As it was with Ardaric, loyalty of the Ostrogoth brothers was first to Attila: 'They ruled in such a way that they respected the dominion of Attila, King of the Huns. Indeed they could not have refused to fight against their kinsmen the Visigoths, and they must even have committed patricide at their lord's command.' Jordanes goes on to say that Valamir was a good keeper of secrets; 'bland of speech and skilled in wiles … Attila might well feel sure that they would fight against the Visigoths, their kinsmen.'

We have no idea how the brothers divided up the leadership of the Ostrogoths at the battle in 451. In all likelihood Valamir had overall command of the left wing with the younger brothers and possibly other lesser Germanic leaders commanding their own followers.

OPPOSING FORCES

NUMBERS

The army Attila led through Germany and into France was probably quite large for the time. Jordanes reports that it was half a million men strong and asserts that there were 165,000 casualties on both sides. Such numbers are impossible. It took a great deal of logistical effort to keep even tens of thousands of men and horses fed and supplied on campaign and for that reason it was rare for armies of this period to exceed 20,000. Larger armies, like the one the Roman emperor Julian had led into Persia nearly a century before, required careful pre-positioning of fodder and supplies.

The actual manpower that could be raised by some of the 5th-century barbarian tribes was nowhere near as great as many fearful Roman writers recounted. The only reasonably reliable numbers we have for a non-Roman army of the period is that of the Vandals who crossed into Africa in AD 429 with 80,000 people. This would give around 10,000 to 15,000 fit and able fighting men. The Huns probably could raise more than that but even so the problems of logistics remained.

Although composed of many contingents it is reasonable to assume that Attila's army contained tens rather than hundreds of thousands of men. This was an invasion force, not a migration, and only the most able warriors would have taken part, leaving others to guard the homelands. In the case of the smaller Germanic contingents it is quite likely that each may have been in the hundreds or low thousands.

As to the Romans, we have no more certainty than we do for the Huns. Jordanes says that Aetius 'assembled warriors from everywhere to meet them

Although Aetius' Romans probably met Hun and Gepid charges with a shieldwall of spears, they would shower their enemies with javelins and light darts before the main clash, as demonstrated by these Spanish re-enactors representing the Legio Septimani Seniores. (Javier Gómez Valero)

(the Huns) on equal terms'. Probably Aetius' combined force outnumbered the Huns slightly. Attila, who had been perfectly happy to take aggressive action in the past, acted quite defensively as soon as the combined Romano-Visigoth army came close which may indicate that they outnumbered him.

We cannot know the exact numbers of each army but a likely and realistic estimate would be something in the region of 20,000–40,000 on each side. As long as Attila's army operated over a large area, kept on the move and looted towns and cities (as it did), supply would not have been an insurmountable problem in late spring/early summer.

Dice games were a popular diversion for soldiers in the ancient world. Most dice were six-sided, making this twelve-sided Roman die, now in the Musée Saint-Loup, rather unique.

AETIUS' ARMY

When Attila crossed the Rhine in the spring of 451, Aetius was in Italy; the latter moved immediately towards Gaul. According to Sidonius Apollinaris, Aetius crossed the Alps leading only 'a thin meagre force of auxiliaries without regular troops'.

It is unclear why more troops from the Italian field army were not released. Quite possibly the emperor did not want to leave Italy undefended, or he did not trust Aetius to have command of too many Roman troops in case he was tempted to stage a coup. There was a famine raging in Italy at that time, which may also have reduced the army's strength and capability.

It is likely that the auxiliaries accompanying Aetius from Italy were not second-rate troops but rather units of *auxilia palatina*, infantry who were capable of standing firm in line of battle as well as conducting more mobile operations. In status and training they were superior to many of the older

These re-enactors from the group Cohors Prima Gallica are equipped as 5th-century Roman infantry. They demonstrate the tight shieldwall formation that would have been adopted to repulse a cavalry charge. (Javier Gómez Valero)

legions and tended to form the backbone of most later West Roman armies. Another interpretation of Sidonius' comment is that the 'auxiliaries' were barbarian allies rather than regular soldiers. Like all generals of the time Aetius would have had at least several hundred *bucellarii*, soldiers who owed their loyalty to the leader directly rather than being part of the regular army. As Aetius had relied almost exclusively on Huns for his support in the past, it is most likely that individual Huns made up the majority of his private bodyguard. Although Aetius was now in conflict with Attila, this would not have necessarily changed the personal loyalty of his Hun *bucellarii*.

Although the men following Aetius into Gaul would have been good troops, there were clearly very few of them, perhaps only a thousand or so and probably a mix of cavalry and infantry. Certainly there were not enough of them to stop Attila by themselves.

Hasty diplomatic actions persuaded the Visigoth king Theodoric to join in an alliance rather than to stay put in southern France to defend his territory. The Visigoths were the descendants of the men who had destroyed the East Roman army at Adrianople in 378 and who had sacked Rome in 410. By this time they had settled down as a warrior aristocracy over the native Gallo-Romans in Aquitaine. They had had access to Roman weapons factories (*fabricae*) for several generations and therefore would have been very well equipped compared to other Germanic peoples.

In the 4th century most Goths fought on foot. By 451 many warriors would have been able to afford horses and they were perfectly happy fighting either mounted or dismounted. On horseback they apparently followed Roman practice. They might use skirmish tactics, riding up to their opponents and showering them with javelins or, if their enemy seemed weaker, charge home with spear and sword. On the defensive the mounted troops would dismount and join the infantry in a shieldwall to fend off attack.

The Visigoths formed a substantial proportion of Aetius' army at the Catalaunian Fields. In reading Jordanes' account we could be forgiven for thinking that they managed to defeat Attila single-handedly. We have no way of knowing how many of them may have been present but it is not unreasonable to assume that they formed something like a third of the total force.

Having linked up with the Visigoths, Aetius then went about gathering up whatever other forces he could raise in Gaul. According to Jordanes: 'He assembled warriors from everywhere to meet [the Huns] on equal terms. Now these were his auxiliaries: Franks, Sarmatians, Armoricans, Liticians, Burgundians, Saxons, Riparians, Olibriones [once Roman soldiers and

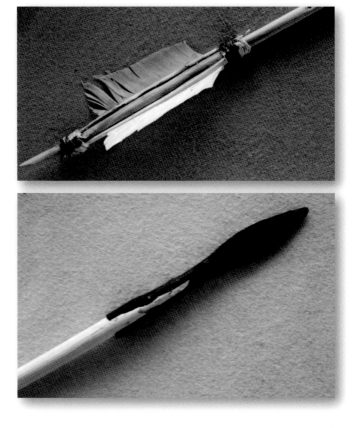

Archery, whether on horse or foot, had become an increasingly important factor in 5th-century warfare. These are examples of migration-period arrows from the Musée des Temps Barbares.

now the flower of the allied forces], and some other Celtic or German tribes.' Interestingly, no mention is made of any Roman troops raised in France. Were there any? The modern historian Hugh Elton maintains that the allies only contributed small contingents and that Aetius' army was mostly made up of regular Roman soldiers. Elton does not however deploy any convincing evidence to support this assertion and the scant contemporary descriptions of the battle indicate that Aetius had very few regular Roman troops.

According to the *Notitia Dignitatum*, a list of Roman offices and units in the early 5th century, the field army of the *Magister Equitum Intra Gallias* contained 12 vexillations of cavalry (300 men each), 10 legions (1,000 men each), 15 *auxilia palatina* (500 men each) and 10 *pseudocomitatenses* (units brought in from frontier garrisons of unknown strength but probably somewhere between 500 and 1,000 men). On paper this should have provided at least 25,000 men. Furthermore there were significant numbers of troops listed as guarding the Rhine frontier. What had happened to them?

The Rhine frontier had collapsed following the migration of the Vandals, Alans and Suebi in 407 and had largely been replaced by settlements of Franks, Alamanni and Burgundians on the west bank of the Rhine. Throughout the 430s and 440s Aetius had relied on Hun and Alan allies rather than the Gallic field army to deal with his enemies and it is quite probable that some of the native Gallo-Roman soldiers either joined or were sympathetic to the Bacaudae. By 451 the Roman army in Gaul had probably been reduced both in numbers and quality to render it almost useless as a field force. Certainly the ease with which Attila captured many Gallic towns with very little resistance is evidence of the paucity of quality troops that could have resisted him. That said, there must have been at least some half-decent Roman soldiers available in Gaul to swell the numbers of Romans Aetius had brought with him from Italy. Possibly the Riparians in Jordanes' description could have been *riparenses*; these were Roman militia, descended from the old legions, who defended river frontiers.

Most Roman troops would have been close-order infantry armed with large oval or round shields, swords and spears. The latter were supplemented with javelins and darts. Vegetius, writing at the end of the 4th century, claimed that Roman infantry had abandoned armour. Although there could have been a lightening of equipment and some units may have

These East Roman soldiers from fragments of the lost Column of Theodosius wear single bowl, plumed, attic-style helmets which are typical of monumental depictions of eastern troops. No examples have been found by archaeology; they contrast to those in the West and along the Danube frontier which have a multi-part construction. Some historians think that these may hark back to classical Greek helmets but the styles are sufficiently different to shed some doubt on this.

suffered from neglect, there is plenty of evidence to show that helmets and body armour continued to be worn. These heavy infantry would have been supported by a small number of foot archers who generally formed the rear ranks, firing overhead. The percentage of cavalry listed in the *Notitia Dignitatum* for the Gallic field army was relatively low (around 10 per cent) but it is reasonable to assume that some Roman cavalry would have been present. Like the Visigoths they would have been spear- and javelin-armed, capable of close combat as well as limited skirmishing.

When Jordanes speaks of 'Sarmatians' he is probably referring to the Alans led by Sangiban as the Alans were a Sarmatian people. In a later passage Jordanes speaks of the Alans 'drawing up a battle-line of heavy armed'. This is confirmed by a reference to the Alans in the life of St Germanus where again they are described as 'armoured cavalry'. Writing in the previous century, Ammianus Marcellinus contradicts this, implying that the Alans were lighter cavalry: 'The Alans are men of great stature and beauty. Their hair is somewhat yellow, their eyes are terribly fierce; the lightness of their armour renders them rapid in their movements, and they are in every respect equal to the Huns, only more civilised in their food and their manner of life.'

Although many Alans were probably originally light horse archers, a large proportion may have been lance-armed cavalry similar to the heavily armoured Sarmatians depicted on Trajan's column. As they had been in Roman service for a generation since Ammianus' time, they would have had access to weapons and equipment from Roman *fabricae*. Horse armour was used by the Sarmatians centuries before and it is not impossible that some of Sangiban's elite followers may have ridden armoured horses. At the Catalaunian Fields the Alans formed a distinct contingent in the centre of the line, indicating a status as allies rather than subordinates.

The Franks in Jordanes' description would have been the supporters of the prince who had turned to the Romans rather than the Huns for help. It is also possible that Jordanes' Riparians refer to a branch of the tribe who later came to be known as the Ripuarian Franks. The Franks were famously foot warriors who preferred to charge in dense columns throwing their axes and heavy javelins before contact and then closing in with hand-to-hand weapons. On the defensive they would form a shieldwall like other Germanic foot warriors. Agathias

For warriors on foot the protruding central iron or bronze boss of their shield was an offensive weapon. These are examples of Frankish weapons now in the Musée Saint-Loup, Troyes.

A depiction of a 5th-century horse archer from a floor mosaic in the Imperial Palace at Constantinople, now the Mosaic Museum Istanbul.

A Frankish belt buckle now in the Musée des Temps Barbares showing a mix of pagan and Christian influences. It probably post-dates the battle but shows the blending of Roman and Germanic cultures.

describes Franks a century later forming a shieldwall when facing enemy cavalry: 'They closed ranks and drew themselves up into a compact formation which, though not deep, was nevertheless a solid mass of shields regularly flanked by the converging wings of cavalry.'

The Armoricans (from modern Brittany) were either Bacaudae, recent immigrants from Britain or a combination of both. The Armorican Bacaudae had been one of Aetius' chief opponents in previous years and possibly they had made a deal with him to provide a contingent in exchange for being left alone to manage their own affairs. Some may have been mounted warriors similar in arms, equipment and tactics to the Visigoths and Romans with their arms being a combination of booty and local manufacture.

Burgundians, settled in Gaul, were the survivors of Aetius' earlier campaign against them and while they had no more cause than the Visigoths or Armoricans to support him, their defeat had come at the hands of the Huns and perhaps they chose the lesser of two evils. The Burgundians most likely fought on foot in a tight shieldwall. The same would have been the case for the Saxons, a band of whom may have been given land to settle north of the Loire. For the Burgundians, the Battle of Campus Mauriacus (the Catalaunian Fields) was so memorable that the *Lex Burgundionum* (Burgundian law) stated that 'All cases which involve Burgundians and which were not completed before the Mauriacian fight [*pugna Mauriacensis*] are declared dismissed.'

The Liticians and Olibriones mentioned by Jordanes are a puzzle. Possibly the Liticians could have been *laeti*, German and Sarmatian military colonists given land in Gaul in return for military service. It is also likely that Aetius' army would have been augmented by the *bucellarii* of the powerful Gallic landowners. Perhaps these could be Jordanes' enigmatic 'Olibriones', especially as Jordanes says that they were previously Roman soldiers. On the other hand this could equally be another description of Roman deserters amongst the Bacaudae.

Most of these contingents were *foederati*, men from a variety of nations who had been given land or pay in return for service in the Roman army. They fought in their native style but were technically part of the Roman army rather than independent allies. They would have been equipped largely from Roman arms factories and may have been almost indistinguishable in appearance from more regular Roman troops.

Aetius' order of battle

Given the paucity of accurate sources, any attempt to construct a detailed order of battle has to be speculative. What follows is a 'best guess' rather than something which should be interpreted as definitive.

The Visigoth contingent comprised 10,000–15,000 men in two commands. The main one, under King Theodoric, held a defensive position, probably dismounted, on the right wing. These would have been a

These re-enactors, from the Legio Prima Germanica group, are equipped as typical late Roman cavalry. The same equipment would have been worn by the Visigoths. (Javier Gómez Valero)

combination of dismounted nobles and other foot, probably supported by a small number of foot archers. A flanking force under Thorismund most likely remained mounted and may have had some light infantry support.

The Alan contingent totalled some 1,000–3,000 men. A combination of horse archers and heavy lance-armed cavalry deployed in the centre of the line, and was commanded by Sangiban. They would have been well equipped as they had been settled in Roman territory for some time, but with low morale as their heart was not in the fight.

The Roman contingent consisted of 10,000–20,000 men. Deployed on the left, the Roman forces comprised several contingents: a small number of high-quality troops brought by Aetius from Italy; the remnants of the Gallic field army supplemented by *laeti* and *riparenses*; Franks; Armoricans; Saxons; and Burgundians. Most would have been infantry fighting in close order and supported by foot archers. A small number, probably held in reserve, may have been cavalry. Aetius had overall command and we do not know who his subordinate commanders were.

This depiction of a horseman from Carthage may well depict an Alan who joined the Vandals in their invasion of Gaul, Spain and then Africa. The tamga brand on the horse's rear is thought to be representative of the Sarmatians and the Alans were a Sarmatian people. (© British Museum)

ATTILA'S ARMY

This Egyptian ivory, now in the Rheinisches Landesmuseum Trier, shows late Roman horse archers armed and equipped as described by the 6th-century writer Procopius. Under the influence of the Huns and Persians, the horse archer became the mainstay of Roman armies shortly after the Battle of Campus Mauriacus.

According to Sidonius Apollinaris:

> Suddenly the barbarian world, rent by a mighty upheaval, poured the whole north into Gaul. After the warlike Rugian comes the fierce Gepid, with the Gelonian close by; the Burgundian urges on the Scirian; forward rush the Hun, the Bellontonian, the Neurian, the Bastarnae, the Thuringian, the Bucteran and the Frank, whose land is washed by the sedgy waters of the Neckar.

There is a huge amount of poetic licence in this description as many of the tribes Sidonius mentions had disappeared centuries before and some are actually fictitious. However, large numbers of Germanic subject and allied contingents did march with the Huns.

Franks fought on both sides at the Battle of Campus Mauriacus. They were renowned for their axes (*franciscae*) which they threw at their enemies just before combat. These examples are from the Musée Saint-Loup, Troyes.

We know one party of the Franks involved in the dynastic dispute had appealed to Attila and so a Frankish contingent is fairly certain. There were also some Burgundians still living to the east of the Rhine and they may have been forced or persuaded to join. The same may have been true of the Alamanni. Although not mentioned in any sources, a number of 5th-century Alamannic graves show that they had adopted the practice of skull deformation from the Huns so a contribution of troops is not unlikely.

Of the other contingents mentioned by Sidonius, the Gepids under Ardaric held the right wing. Rugians, Thuringians and Scirians were East German tribes who lived under Hun overlordship so their inclusion in Attila's army is probable. It is also quite likely that a contingent of Heruls, who at that time were living near the Black Sea, may also have been present. Interestingly Sidonius does not mention the Ostrogoths, although they are conspicuous in Jordanes' account of the battle, forming the left wing.

The Huns were famously mounted archers, armed with powerful composite bows and skilled at loosing off a swarm of arrows while avoiding contact until their enemy had been worn down or had lost cohesion. However, they were also quite prepared to charge in to close combat so it would be a mistake to think of them as purely light cavalry skirmishers.

The 4th-century Roman officer Ammianus Marcellinus gives an excellent description of their fighting methods:

> They enter the battle drawn up in wedge-shaped masses, while their medley of voices makes a savage noise. And as they are lightly equipped for swift motion, and unexpected in action, they purposely divide suddenly into scattered bands and attack, rushing about in disorder here and there, dealing terrific slaughter … then they gallop over the intervening spaces and fight hand-to-hand with swords, regardless of their own lives; and while the enemy are guarding against wounds from the sabre-thrusts, they throw strips of cloth plaited into nooses over their opponents and so entangle them that they fetter their limbs and take from them the power of riding or walking.

An elaborate Visigoth horse bit from Spain. Although it post-dates the Battle of Campus Mauriacus, such bits may have been in use earlier. (Javier Gómez Valero)

Such tactics gave the Huns an almost unbroken string of success against their Roman and Germanic opponents who had no answer to the effect of massed horse archery followed up with aggressive charges. The physical and psychological effect of a whirlwind of men galloping up, firing arrows, then swerving away only to be replaced by others, would have been devastating to men unused to such tactics.

Lajos Kassai, a modern Hungarian horse archery expert, has taught himself to fire 6 arrows in 10 seconds at the gallop with incredible accuracy. Imagine this multiplied many times over. A unit of 1,000 men could gallop towards the enemy at a speed of around 30–40km/h; open fire at 150m; shoot again at 100m; split right and left at around 40–50m to ride parallel to the line, firing once or twice more before turning away and shooting to the rear. In the space of only a few seconds they could easily have loosed off 5,000–6,000 aimed arrows on a relatively narrow front. The impact would have been devastating. It would have pinned their opponents behind their shields making them an ideal target for a well-timed charge before they could recover.

A modern Hungarian horse archer demonstrates the way Hun horse archers would have fought. Lajos Kassai has shown how it is possible to fire six arrows in ten seconds at the gallop with incredible accuracy. (Csanády)

Like the English longbowmen many centuries later, this would have required a great deal of training. It took Lajos four years to teach himself to fire so fast and accurately, but then every Hun boy would have been training from the moment he was born and had the added benefit of many mentors to help him. It is perhaps no wonder that the Huns had been held in such high regard by Aetius and that in the years that followed the Romans developed a horse archer-based army.

In contrast to the Huns, the various Germanic subjects favoured hand-to-hand combat, either on horse or foot. Those Germans who had been living out on the steppes for a long time were more likely to have fought mounted.

These belt buckles from the mid-5th century Pouan treasure found near the Catalaunian Plains battlefield show the craftsmanship that went into the panoply of a 5th-century warrior.

These would have included the Ostrogoths, Gepids, Heruls and possibly the Scirians. Their tactics are described in the *Strategikon*, a 6th-century East Roman military manual: 'They lean forward, cover their heads and part of their horses' necks with their shields, hold their lances high as their shoulders.' Unlike the Visigoths, who used a combination of skirmish and shock tactics when mounted, some of these eastern Germans may have adopted the use of very long two-handed lances from the Sarmatians for shock action only.

Those Germans living further west, such as the Franks, Burgundians, Alamanni, Thuringians and Rugians, probably fought mostly on foot. Depending on the circumstances they might either charge in dense columns or form a tight shieldwall if fighting defensively.

Both the Huns and the Germans had been living in close contact with the Romans for several generations and in recent years the Huns had won significant victories over the East Romans. By 451 most of them would have worn Roman clothing and equipment and supplemented their native weapons with those they had appropriated from the Romans. The popular mental image of Huns in furs and skins with Mongolian style head dress is probably quite wrong for the men who followed Attila. It is far more likely that they wore Roman-style clothing with helmets and armour looted from the battlefield or acquired from the vast sums paid to them as tribute from Constantinople.

This 5th-century horse ornament may depict a Hun warrior.

This silver dish from Isola Rizza probably shows a 6th-century East Roman soldier riding down a Lombard. Many men in both Aetius' and Attila's army would have looked quite similar. (James Steakley)

The passage previously quoted, describing the encounter between Avitus and Huns in the service of Litorius, says that the Hun's body armour was split open. In another passage Sidonius mentions how the Huns practiced skull deformation by binding the heads of children so that they grew into an elongated shape. He misinterprets this as being done so that young men would better fit a helmet with a nose guard: 'The nostrils, while soft are blunted by an encircling band, to proven the nose from growing outward between the cheekbones, that thus they make room for helmets' (Sidonius Apollinaris, panegyric on Avitus). This is wrong as it was the forehead that was constricted and several female Hun skulls have been found that had been deformed in the same way. However, it is an indication that men such as Sidonius, who were familiar with the Huns, expected them to wear helmets – most probably of segmented 'Spangenhelm' style with nose and cheek guards.

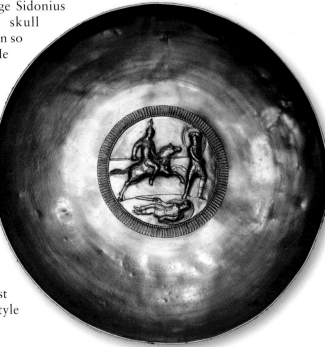

Not all Attila's followers would have been armoured. The Heruls, who had little contact with Rome at this time, were noted by Jordanes as being 'lightly armed'. A century later Procopius said that they 'have neither helmet nor corselet nor any other protective armour except a shield and a thick jacket.'

Attila's order of battle

As with Aetius' army, a detailed breakdown of Attila's forces is impossible. Even the rough proportion of each contingent has to be guessed at. None of the sources give any indication of where the smaller Germanic tribes formed up. They could have been split between the wings, or possibly those on foot formed a second line for the cavalry to rally back on.

The Ostrogoth contingent comprised 5,000–10,000 men. Holding the left flank, the Ostrogoths were probably under Valamir's overall command. They were primarily mounted troops favouring shock tactics, probably supported by a number of foot archers and other foot warriors including some of those from the smaller allied contingents.

The Hun contingent consisted of 10,000–15,000 men, all of whom would have been well-equipped horse archers capable and willing to fight hand-to-hand as well as shoot from a distance. Most would probably have worn some body armour. The majority were deployed in the centre of the line but a covering force contested the high ground with the Visigoths as a prelude to the main battle. Attila had overall command and most likely his sons Ellac, Dengizic and Ernac would have held subordinate commands.

The Gepid contingent totalled 5,000–10,000 men. Ardaric, King of the Gepids, formed the right wing. In all likelihood he commanded a number of other Germanic allies as well as his own men. The Gepids were probably mostly mounted warriors similar to the Ostrogoths while the Franks and others fought on foot.

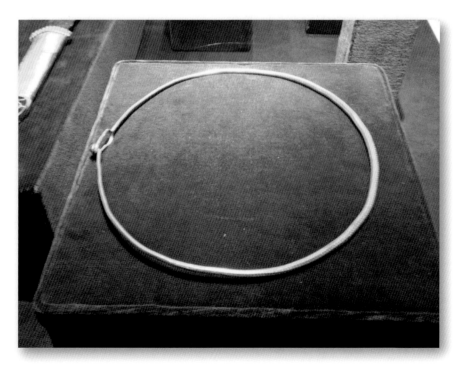

Neck rings like this gold example from the Pouan treasure were the mark of a warrior. They were worn by Celtic warriors fighting Julius Caesar and continued to be worn in the 5th century AD by Germans fighting both for and against Rome.

THE CAMPAIGN

Attila crossed the Rhine in the spring of 451. He had a large army at his back and keeping it fed and watered would have been a monumental task. To do so he had to keep on the move, probably splitting his force into smaller bands to make foraging easier and then congregating to threaten a town and hopefully forcing it to open its gates and its granaries.

Food and water were not his only considerations. Attila's polyglot army followed him because they believed he would lead them to victory and riches. His supporters would start to melt away if they found themselves on a long drawn-out campaign on short rations and with no loot. Therefore Attila had to balance the benefits to be gained by capturing a town against the dangers of becoming bogged down in a long siege.

The massive, well-preserved late Roman walls of Sens were not breached by Attila, even though he passed the town on his way to Orléans and on his retreat back.

Attila's invasion of Gaul. The exact route taken by Attila is not known beyond the fact that he took Metz in April and was at Orléans by June. The arrows show the central axis of his march. Most probably his forces split up and foraged widely over the countryside. It is also not certain whether Aetius and Theodoric joined forces before marching on Orléans or whether they moved independently, as shown on this map.

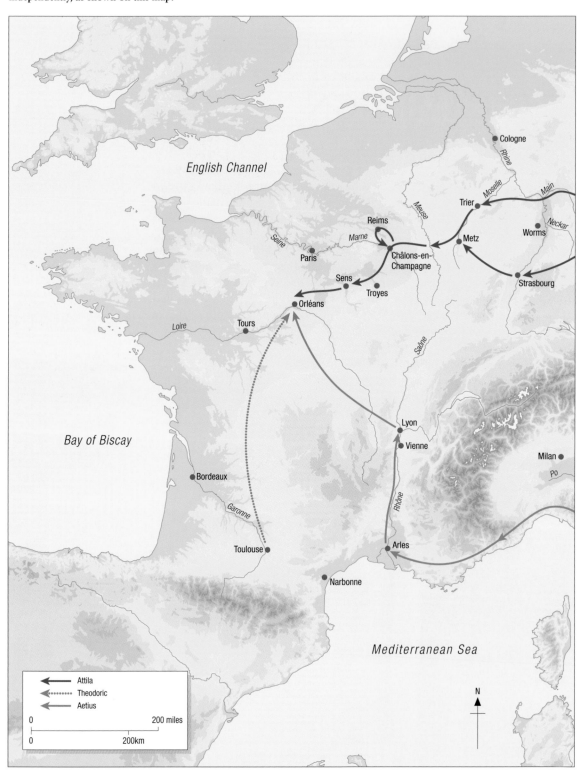

VIRGINS, BISHOPS AND SAINTS

The Huns captured and sacked Metz on 7 April 451. What they did then is far from clear. Gregory of Tours tells us that 'Attila king of the Huns went forth from Metz and crushed many cities of the Gauls'. The *Chronicle of Hydatius* states: 'The tribe of the Huns broke the peace treaty, pillaged the province of Gaul, and sacked a vast number of cities.' Which cities they actually sacked or tried to sack is shrouded in early Christian legend with various saints either being given credit for saving their cities from the ravages of the Huns or becoming martyrs. Rheims, Mainz, Strasbourg, Cologne, Worms and Trier are all said to have fallen to Attila, which may or may not have been the case.

Perhaps the most famous of these Christian legends is the story of St Geneviève. In a striking parallel to the later legends of Jeanne d'Arc, Geneviève was a peasant girl who had frequent visions of heavenly saints and angels and went on to save Paris (although not all of France), first from the Huns and later the Franks. Under the patronage of Germanus, Bishop of Auxerre, she moved to Paris and dedicated herself to God. This pious woman is said to have urged the people to stay and resist rather than abandoning the city to the Huns. As the legend goes, Geneviève told the frightened Parisians that if they kept their faith, fasted, prayed and did penance, the city would be protected by God and their lives would be spared. Naturally there were some doubters and several citizens turned against her. However, Geneviève was supported by Germanus' archdeacon, who may have been sent from Italy to help calm things. If true, this shows that panic had been spreading long before Attila crossed the Rhine and the religious as well as temporal authorities at Ravenna took action to shore up Gaul's defences.

The route from Orléans to Troyes is characterised by hilly, wooded terrain which would not have been suitable for Attila's cavalry-based army. Therefore he fell back to the open fields of Champagne then known as the Catalaunian Fields. The terrain offered plenty of opportunities for delaying actions by Attila's Gepid rearguard.

One version of the story has it that as Attila approached Paris, Geneviève led a group of women outside the walls of the city to pray for deliverance. Attila was so impressed that he did not attack. It may be that Geneviève's actions did prevent an exodus from the city and possibly Attila would have taken Paris if it had been abandoned. It is just as likely, however, that he had already decided to bypass Paris to move against Orléans.

All we know for certain is that from April to June 451 Attila's army cut a swathe through northern France from Metz to Orléans. They probably operated over a very wide area in relatively small bands to ease problems of supply and forage. Without any decent standing Roman forces to oppose them, they would have been able to move through the countryside more or less at will with logistics dictating their movements as much or more than tactical considerations. Capturing a city would have given the Huns loot, slaves and supplies but they could not afford protracted siege operations. They would have depended on fear to open city gates, offering to spare the inhabitants from the horrors of a sack in exchange for food, supplies and shelter. If the gates remained closed, the Huns may have tried an assault provided that they thought their chances were good, otherwise they would bypass and move on.

The inability of barbarians to conduct a siege is well known but probably over-exaggerated. Attila had many Greek and Roman advisors and certainly there were engineers amongst them who could oversee the building of siege engines. The Huns had successfully besieged and captured many cities in the Eastern Empire in the 440s so it was not technical inability that might prevent a successful siege of a Gallic city in 451. What Attila could not afford was to get bogged down at a single place for any length of time when the logistical problems of keeping and feeding a large army would have become insurmountable.

Ideally Attila wanted to reward his followers with loot while creating such a nuisance that Aetius would have no choice other than to sue for peace. In the worst case he would force the Romans to offer battle, defeat them as he had done so often in the East and then extract terms. What he had not counted on was a formidable Romano-Visigoth alliance that could stand up to him.

By the 5th century most Roman soldiers resembled a part-time militia. They tended their plots of land and would fight to defend their locality if called on. However, the mobile field forces were increasingly made up of Germans, Alans and Huns. (Javier Gómez Valero)

The Romans needed time to put this alliance together and forge an army capable of stopping Attila. To do this they encouraged the inhabitants of the walled cities to hold firm and bar their gates to the enemy thus denying them much needed supplies. It seems as though this task fell primarily to the ecclesiastical authorities.

There is no shortage of stories of saintly bishops shoring up the resolve of their congregations to resist Attila. Some were successful and others became martyrs. Bishop Nicasius of Reims was allegedly killed and the city pillaged. According to legend the bishop's sister Eutropia, a pious virgin, stood up to the Huns and scratched out Attila's eyes before being killed herself as she sought refuge in a church. However, another version of the story has Nicasius being killed by the Vandals in 407 and yet another has him dying of smallpox. Many such stories mix up previous events with Attila's invasion. Amongst these are the stories of St Servatius of Tongeren and St Diogenes of Arras, both of whom had been dead for some time, making their intervention against Attila highly improbable despite their sanctity!

The legend of St Ursula is probably one of the most fanciful stories to emerge from Attila's invasion of Gaul. Here Ursula, a virtuous British princess, travels to Cologne to be married. She is accompanied by 11 virgin handmaidens (later expanded in the middle ages to 11,000) and all are killed when the Huns destroy the city. Despite a late Roman inscription on the Church of St Ursula in Cologne and the medieval discovery of the bones of several children which came to be revered as the relics of the 11,000 virgins, there is probably little truth to the story. Most of the details were invented in the Middle Ages, and another version of the St Ursula legend places the events a century or more beforehand. There is indeed some doubt as to whether or not Cologne was even attacked by Attila in 451.

The Roman road from Sens to Troyes follows the River Vanne, which would have provided an ample source of water for both Attila's and Aetius' armies.

The hilt and scabbard of the long sword from the treasure of Pouan at the Musée Saint-Loup, Troyes. Such weapons would have been carried by notable men on both sides of the conflict.

The source of the Vanne at the modern hamlet of Fontvannes. This is the last water source before reaching the Seine above Troyes.

On the other hand, St Lupus, the Bishop of Troyes (Tricassium), was real and his actions probably had a significant impact on the battle. According to legend, Lupus confronted Attila outside the walls of Troyes. Dressed in his full regalia he asked Attila who he was. Attila is famously said to have replied that he was the 'scourge of God' (*fagellum dei*), an epithet which has stayed with him to this day bringing vivid images of barbaric savagery to modern minds. The ancients, however, saw it somewhat differently. The horror of invasion was widely interpreted by the early Church as God's punishment for their sins. If a city was sacked, it was God's righteous wrath; if it was spared, it was due to the timely intervention of a saint. In response to Attila, Bishop Lupus is supposed to have responded that if the Hun was 'the scourge of God and the hammer with which Providence smites the earth', then he should do only God's will. Attila is supposed to have been so impressed that he spared the city.

Local folklore in Troyes has Lupus confronting and slaying a dragon which had been devastating the region and killing many children. For over a millennium this was celebrated each year when the dragon of the *chair salée* (salted flesh) was paraded through the city. The origins of the festival are variously explained either as St Lupus defeating the Pelagian heresy or defeating Attila. The festival was banned in 1727 but it has been revived in modern times.

What probably happened is that Lupus offered Attila a deal, providing supplies and pasture in exchange for sparing the city. Troyes lies on the Seine at the junction of two important Roman roads. One is the Via Agrippa from Lyon to Boulogne, the other road runs from Le Havre to Troyes by way of Paris and Sens. If Attila had indeed sacked Reims and then intended to move on to Orléans, his best route would have been to cut south through the open Catalaunian Fields (modern Champagne) towards Troyes and then head west along the road that passed through Sens and on to Orléans. This route would have provided ample grazing for Attila's many horses with the Seine and its tributaries giving them a vital water supply. By securing Troyes and the surrounding region as a neutral if not friendly refuge, Attila would have been able to concentrate his forces, rest, recoup and resupply for a push on Orléans. A deal which gave him this without a siege would have been worth taking. For Lupus, giving up some of the city's wealth in exchange for sparing it from the horrors of a sack would have made him seem like a saviour to the terrified inhabitants.

What we do not know for certain is whether the encounter between Attila and Lupus happened en route to Orléans, or on the way back. According to the *Lives of the Saints*, Attila took Lupus back with him across the Rhine as a hostage after the battle. Later when he returned Lupus went into exile, possibly as a result of suspicion falling on him for collaboration with Attila. This, combined with the fact that Troyes would have made a very good stopping point on the route, leads to the conclusion that Attila made his deal with Lupus on the way to Orléans. He may even have established a supply base at Troyes before moving westward.

Although it is a fairly straight line on the map from Metz to Orléans by way of Troyes, tracing the exact route the Huns took from April to June 451 is impossible. It is most likely that there were several routes with small bands moving more or less independently, ravaging the countryside, capturing what towns they could and then moving on.

THE SIEGE OF ORLÉANS

In early June 451, Attila concentrated his forces on Orléans. This may have been at the invitation of Sangiban, the Alan leader, who had promised to turn the city over to him. On the other hand it may have simply been part of a plan to cut Gaul in half from the Rhine to the Atlantic and Sangiban thought that by helping the Huns he would be joining the winning side. What actually happened at Orléans is not entirely clear. If we are to believe the stories of the saints then Attila besieged the city but failed to capture it due to divine intervention.

Gregory of Tours recounts that Attila 'attacked Orléans and strove to take it by the mighty hammering of battering rams.' According to the legend of the Bishop Anianus of Orléans, the Huns deployed siege engines and battering rams against the city, although they were delayed for several days due to unseasonable weather. Bishop Anianus prayed as the garrison was driven from the walls and the gates began to give way. Just as all seemed lost, the good bishop sent an attendant to the walls to see if he could see anything. Twice the messenger reported back that there was nothing to be seen. On the symbolic third time 'like the messenger of Elijah' he saw a cloud of dust in the distance. Just as the Huns were beginning to force a breach, with the women wailing and the hapless inhabitants cowering in anticipation of 'terrible chastisement', the army of Goths and Romans came into view and Attila was forced to break off the siege.

The flat ground by source of the Vanne was the probable campsite of Aetius' army the night before the battle. No doubt Attila would have used the same spot a day or two before.

This version of events is disputed by the historian J. B. Bury, who believes that Aetius and Theodoric reached Orléans before Attila and therefore no siege took place. The narrative of Jordanes says as much: 'Sangiban, king of the Alans, smitten with fear of what might come to pass, had promised to surrender to Attila, and to give into his keeping Aureliani [Orléans], a city of Gaul wherein he dwelt. When Theodoric and Aetius learned of this, they cast up great earthworks around that city before Attila's arrival and kept watch over the suspected Sangiban.'

Bishop Anianus probably did much to keep up the hopes and spirits of the alarmed inhabitants in the knowledge that Aetius and Theodoric were on their way. The arrival of the allies in time to save the city could easily be interpreted as an answer to his prayers. Not letting reality stand in the way of a good story, it probably did the Church no harm to magnify the danger and augment the services of the saintly bishop by representing the enemy as already battering down the gates. In one account we are told that Anianus actually travelled to Arles to meet with Aetius and help plan the campaign before Attila's move on Orléans.

Either way, Attila fell back from Orléans, probably in early June. It may be that he had attempted a siege and was forced to lift it on Aetius' arrival, but it is more likely that he got there only to find Aetius and Theodoric already in place with Sangiban having switched sides. Whatever the case, Attila had three choices: fight at Orléans, fall back to make a stand elsewhere, or withdraw altogether. In reality the last choice was not an option. Having gathered and led a huge army into the Western Empire with promises of land, booty and honour, Attila could not possibly now turn back simply because the combined Roman-Gothic foes that opposed him were stronger than he may have anticipated. His strength rested on the belief that he would bring his followers wealth, victory and honour. To give up now would destroy the myth of invincibility and fracture his power base.

This reconstruction of 3rd-century Troyes shows what the town would have looked like at the time of the battle.

A fight at Orléans would have favoured the Roman-Visigoths rather than the Huns. If we believe Jordanes, Aetius had entrenched positions around the city. The Romans and Goths had good, well-equipped infantry while the strength of the Huns and their allies was in mounted action, which required open terrain with room to manoeuvre. Attila had knowledge of the ground that he had crossed to reach Orléans and he would certainly have been aware that the flat open region of modern Champagne, or the Catalaunian Fields as Jordanes calls it, would favour his army over that of his opponents. Therefore he withdrew from Orléans and fell back on Troyes.

There is some evidence to suggest that Attila was quite unsettled by finding himself suddenly opposed by a combined Romano-Visigoth alliance and faced with an army that possibly outnumbered his own. Jordanes recounts: 'Attila, king of the Huns, was taken aback by this event and lost confidence in his own troops, so that he feared to begin the conflict.' This is probably an over-exaggeration made with the benefit of hindsight and to stress a moral ascendancy of the Goths over the Huns. With Sangiban's anticipated support, Attila had expected Orléans would have fallen to him without a fight. Now that this was not possible, he had no choice but to fight Aetius and Theodoric, but he wanted to do this on ground of his own choosing.

It is likely that Aetius gathered in further reinforcements before following up Attila's withdrawal. There is a possibility that the Franks supporting Aetius were already a band in exile serving with the Roman army and could possibly have marched with him from Italy. Otherwise it is hard to conceive that they would have cut across Attila's lines to join with the Visigoths in southern France before Aetius reached Orléans. The Saxons may have been settled in the Loire Valley and it is unlikely that they would have committed to Aetius' cause unless he was in the vicinity and looking like he might win. Sangiban's Alans had been given land around Orléans to keep the Armorican

The ground to the east of Troyes is wide open and perfectly flat – the perfect place for Attila to offer battle.

Bacaudae in check and Orléans was the gateway to Bacaudae territory. Only Aetius' presence and a promise of autonomy would have persuaded the Armoricans to join the fight. There is no possibility that any them would have been part of Aetius' army before his arrival there. The other known Roman allies were the Burgundians of Savoy. Given their more southerly location it is possible that they had already joined Aetius at Arles rather than linking up with him at Orléans.

It is about 200km from Troyes to Orléans. According to Vegetius, a Roman army 'should march with the common military step twenty miles in five summer-hours, and with the full step, which is quicker, twenty-four miles in the same number of hours.' Assuming Attila's mostly mounted force could accomplish the same, this is less than a two-week march, even if encumbered with loot and having to forage along the way. If Attila had stopped to gather his forces at Troyes before pushing on to Orléans, he would not have started that march if he knew that Aetius and Theodoric were already there. Therefore Aetius could not have arrived at Orléans more than a few days before Attila. If so, he probably had to wait a while longer to gather in his new allies rather than following immediately with all his forces as the Huns fell back.

ATTILA'S RETREAT FROM ORLÉANS

Disengaging from a well-formed enemy and withdrawing over difficult terrain is a tricky business at the best of times. Yet this is what Attila had to do if he wanted to fight on ground of his choosing. The route from Orléans back to the open plains of Champagne passes through what are now known as the Forêt d'Orléans and the Forêt d'Othe – hilly wild territory with little room to manoeuvre and few choices for alternative passages. Attila would have had the added challenge of keeping his army's morale up, no doubt by reminding them of the favourable terrain around Troyes, promising to make a stand there and assuring them that victory was certain.

As he had passed through Champagne before moving to Orléans, Attila knew that the flat open ground there favoured his army over the Romano-Visigoths. The Catalaunian Fields, as Champagne was then known, took its name from Duro Catalaunum (modern Châlons-en-Champagne). It is an

This is the view from the ridge of Montgueux looking east towards the Seine where a line of trees in the distance mark its passage. This is the view Aetius would have had as he reached the heights on the morning of 20 June 451.

Attila's retreat from Orléans. Attila's options would have been limited as he fell back from the close terrain around Orléans to the open plains by Troyes. Although his infantry may have been able to make their way cross-country through the Forêt d'Orléans, his baggage would have kept to the road. It is possible that Aetius had to delay a few days at Orléans to gather in more allies before following up with his main force.

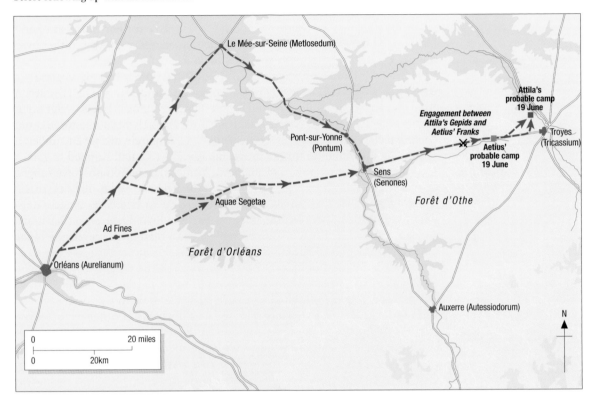

area which, as Jordanes explained, 'extended in length one hundred leagues, as the Gauls express it, and seventy in width.' There Attila's cavalry would have room to manoeuvre and his horse archers could wreak havoc on his less mobile opponents.

To get there Attila really had only one option: the Roman road that runs parallel to the River Vanne, passing by Sens (Senones) and then on to Troyes. His main axis of retreat must have been along that road. The Vanne would have

given him a good source of water and the Roman road would have allowed the passage of his wagons. Where he could, Attila probably split his forces to move on as wide an area as possible to avoid a long snaking convoy that could be easily held up and be vulnerable to attack, and to make foraging less difficult.

By the time they reached Sens, the dense terrain of the Forêt d'Othe would have forced the Huns to keep to the single road running parallel to the River Vanne. In stark contrast to the flat, open farmland between Troyes and Châlons-en-Champagne, the modern Route Nationale D660, which follows the old Roman road, winds its way through hills and forest. The impressive Roman walls of Sens still stand today and there is no indication that they were ever breached by Attila. Time would have been of the essence and even if Sens could have afforded him a welcome source of supplies, Attila could not have spared the time even to intimidate the inhabitants to open the gates to him.

Attila was able to make a clean break from Orléans. Aetius no doubt sent troops after him to harass his retreat but if the Romans had to wait to gather in their new allies, they would not have been able to follow up immediately with their entire army in hot pursuit. However, Attila's retreat was not entirely unhindered. Our sources tell us that there was an engagement between the Gepids of Attila's rearguard and the Franks of Aetius' vanguard, which resulted in an unlikely 15,000 casualties. According to Jordanes this engagement took place the day before the main battle. We do not know where this engagement took place or even if it was the only one on the retreat from Orléans. There are plenty of wooded, hilly ridges from Sens to Troyes where Attila could easily have deployed a delaying force to hinder pursuit and where the close terrain would have lent itself to success. The Gepids were probably mounted but, like most Germanic warriors, were perfectly happy

Attila would have camped somewhere along the River Seine to the north of Troyes, where he could have established an easily defensible camp with ample water and forage.

dismounting to fight on foot when the situation demanded. They could have set up a shieldwall, perhaps supported by archers, and inflicted long delays on Aetius' Franks before mounting up again and pulling back to establish a new defensive position. Such rearguard actions would have bought valuable time for Attila. They would have created enough separation between his main army and that of Aetius so that he would not be caught in the close terrain of the Forêt d'Othe before reaching the open plains around Troyes.

Less than a day's march from Troyes would have found Attila at the modern hamlet of Fontvannes, the source of the River Vanne. This was the last place he could have camped with a good supply of water before pushing on to the Seine. From here he had two routes open to him. He could either go directly east along the Roman road to Troyes or cut across the hills through a valley that would bypass Troyes and meet up with the Seine just to the north of the city. In all probability his large army would have taken all available routes.

The *Life of Saint Lupus* leads us to understand that Attila retired by several roads at once before converging on Troyes. No doubt some of his troops branched off to the north-east heading in a direct line to the River Seine just to the north of Troyes. Here they could have established a camp with an excellent water source, plenty of grazing for their horses and food supplies from the city on the assumption that Bishop Lupus was living up to his agreement. Others, especially the baggage train, would have kept to the Roman road until they reached the outskirts of Troyes and then moved around the city to rejoin the others.

The most likely spot for Attila's camp is somewhere near the modern village of Saint-Lyé just to the north of Troyes. Here there was plenty of space for his wagons to form a large laager on the banks of the Seine with 7km of flat open plains to his front extending as far as the eye could see to the left and right. This would give him advance warning of any enemy approach, time to deploy and wide open spaces for manoeuvre. There is also evidence of an ancient bridge that crossed the Seine at this point, giving an additional avenue of escape if things went badly.

Aetius would have been following up Attila's retreat as hard and fast as he could. His advance elements would have been harassing the Hun rearguard while the bulk of the army followed up behind. The Romano-Visigoths would have suffered less from logistical problems than the Huns. They would have been able to resupply at Sens as well as at Orléans and although the Roman commissariat was not what it had been in previous centuries, Aetius' army

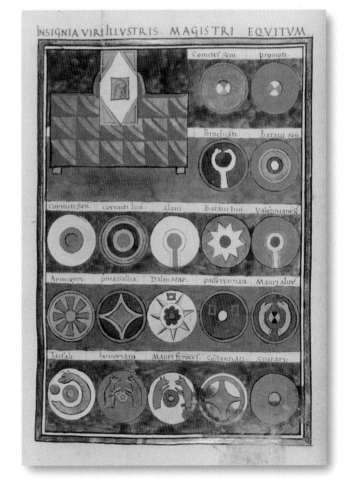

The insignia of the *Magistri Equitum* showing the shield patterns of the senior Roman units at the outset of the 5th century. In theory they should have been available to Aetius to call on to defend Gaul. In reality many or most of these units were probably so run down as to be nearly useless in an offensive campaign. (Bodleian Library, Oxford)

This 5th-century wood carving from Egypt, now in the Museum für Byzantinische Kunst, Berlin, shows late Roman soldiers defending a city from marauding tribesmen. Although the garrisons of Gallic cities had been run down, if the defenders held their nerve they could keep the Huns at bay, as the latter could not afford to get bogged down in a long siege.

had not been living off the land for the past three months like Attila's.

It is impossible to say how many days' march Aetius' main body was behind Attila's. Even if he had paused for a while at Orléans to gather more allies, Aetius' advance guard was certainly hard on Attila's heels given the engagement between his Franks and Attila's Gepids along the route. However close he may have been, Aetius would have had to stop for at least a day to gather his forces together and issue orders for the attack. An army of around 20,000–40,000 men, compelled by difficult terrain to follow a single road, would have taken a long time to gather together. The column would have been at least 10km long, probably longer taking into account gaps between contingents and space for baggage wagons. Therefore as the first men were arriving at the new location, the rearguard would barely have set off from their previous night's camp.

The only possible place short of Troyes where Aetius could have gathered his army together was at Fontvannes. Here there was sufficient space, water and forage. Further back the terrain was too close to gather a large army and further forward there was plenty of space but no water until the Seine where Attila was already waiting for him.

It is just over 8km from Fontvannes to high ground overlooking the plains around Troyes. Jordanes tells us that the battle started at the 'ninth hour of the day'. He goes on to explain that this was a late start as Attila was fearful of the result and hoped that 'impending darkness might come to his aid if the outcome should be disastrous.' This most probably means nine hours after dawn, or about one in the afternoon rather than nine in the morning. This late start is more easily accounted for by the time it would have taken Aetius to move his army from Fontvannes to a position overlooking Attila's lines above the modern village of Grange-l'Evêque rather than insecurity on Attila's part. Setting off at dawn, Aetius and Theodoric could have reached the heights above the modern hamlet of Grange-l'Evêque, 7km from Attila's camp on the banks of the Seine, and deployed their army ready for battle shortly after noon.

Attila's light cavalry scouts would have been shadowing Aetius' movements. As soon as he was aware that Aetius was deploying for battle, Attila would have marshalled his host in the wide open plains around Troyes and prepared to meet the enemy.

THE BATTLE

THE BATTLEFIELD

'The armies met … in the Catalaunian Fields. The battlefield was a plain rising by a sharp slope to a ridge, which both armies sought to gain; for advantage of position is a great help' (Jordanes). This is the most detailed description we have of the battlefield. It is not much to go on and, to quote the modern historian Arther Ferrill, searching for the exact location has 'been a favourite occupation of retired colonels for many years'.

The clash between Aetius and Attila is commonly called the 'Battle of Châlons'. This results from Jordanes saying that it took place in the Catalaunian Fields. The modern city of Châlons-en-Champagne was called Duro Catalaunum in Roman times. The Catalaunian Fields must, therefore, take its name from Châlons-en-Champagne. However, earlier in his account Jordanes says that the armies met 'in the Catalaunian Fields, which are also called Mauriacian, extending in length 100 leagues, as the Gauls express it, and 70 in width. Now a Gallic league measures a distance of 1,500 paces.' So Jordanes' description is generic rather than specific. An area 150,000 paces long and 105,000 wide is hardly a pinpoint location. Rather it is an area that equates to the plains of modern Champagne with Châlons-en-Champagne at the northern end and Troyes about 80km further south.

As Aetius neared the heights above the Catalaunian Fields, he would have seen the ridge off to his right which was probably occupied by rearguard detachments of Attila's army. Therefore he tasked Thorismund to drive off the enemy, possibly accompanying the Goths himself.

Jordanes gives the alternate name of Mauriacus or Maurica, which is also used by Gregory of Tours and other Gallic chroniclers. The unknown continuator of the *Chronicle of Prosper* is quite specific about where this is: 'The battle takes place five miles [8km] from Troyes at a place called Maurica in Champagne.' For five miles the ground to the west of Troyes is absolutely flat but then it rises up to a sharp ridge now called Montgueux. This is just as Jordanes describes the battlefield.

Writing in the *Revue Historique* in 1885, M. Girard observed that in his day the area around Montgueux was known as 'les Maures' and that there was a road running north-west from Troyes known as the 'Voie des Maures'. Even today modern French maps name the flat farmland between Montgueux and Troyes as 'les Maurattes'. There are further indications that long forgotten memories of the battle still exist in modern place names. The area just at the foot of the ridge is called 'l'Enfer' or 'hell'. If the ridge of Montgueux is indeed the ridge from which Thorismund's Visigoths charged down into the flank of Attila's army, then 'hell' would be an appropriate name. Jordanes says that a brook 'flowing between low banks through the plain was greatly increased by blood from the wounds of the slain. It was not flooded by showers, as brooks usually rise, but was swollen by a strange stream and turned into a torrent by the increase of blood.' There is indeed a small stream running towards Troyes from the west and the area surrounding it, now an industrial estate, is today called 'la Rivière de Corps' (the river of bodies).

Is there any possibility, however, that the battle could have taken place near Châlons-en-Champagne and therefore be legitimately called the Battle of Châlons?

The area to the south of Châlons-en-Champagne is open and relatively flat, although there are more undulations than the perfectly flat plain to the west of Troyes. It would have been suitable for Attila's cavalry but not quite as good as the latter. Just over 30km south-west of Châlons-en-Champagne there is indeed a prominent piece of high ground near the modern town of Vertus. It is known today as Le Mont Aimé and it completely dominates the plains below. Unlike Montgueux near Troyes, it is a high hill rather than a ridge and its slopes are very steep. Troops on the heights of Mont Aimé would have had to pick their way carefully down the sides of the hill and could not have charged down with anything like the impact that Thorismund could have done on the relatively gentle slope of the Montgueux ridge. There are remnants of medieval fortifications at the top of Mont Aimé, built on top of Carolingian works which in turn are renovations of Roman defences. If this was a known fortified site then we might have expected at least one ancient historian to mention it by name, but this is not the case.

This stele, now in the Hermitage Museum, St Petersburg, is thought to represent an Alan. Such men fought under Sangiban in the centre of the Romano-Visigoth array.

The strategic situation also argues against the battle taking place close to Châlons-en-Champagne. To reach the latter on his retreat from Orléans, Attila would have had to first fall back on Troyes and then head north along the eastern bank of the Seine for another 80km. Why would he have done this when the terrain around Troyes was so perfectly suited for open cavalry action and he had an agreement with Bishop Lupus to supply him?

What then of archaeological evidence? Unfortunately there is very little. The only significant discovery is the 'treasure of Pouan'. Uncovered in 1842, this magnificent find is now displayed in the Musée Saint-Loup at Troyes. It consists of two swords and various pieces of gold jewellery including a signet ring engraved with the name Heva. Dated to the second half of the 5th century the decoration of the swords are of Western origin while other items show Danubian influences. Initially it was thought that these may have been the grave goods of King Theodoric but this is now generally discounted. It is unlikely that the Visigoths would have buried their king near the battlefield rather than taking the body back to Toulouse. Possibly, given the mixed Western and Eastern origins of the artefacts, the treasure of Pouan could have come from the grave of one of Attila's notable followers. Pouan is just 40km to the north-east of the probable battlefield and could well have been on the route of Attila's withdrawal. On the other hand some archaeologists argue that the items are from a few years after the battle and may have nothing to do with it at all. However, such a significant find from about the right time and so close to the battlefield does give pause for thought.

One other possible site for the battle given by modern historians is near the village of Méry-sur-Seine, 30km north-west of Troyes. This is because of the proximity to Pouan and the possibility that the name Méry could be derived from 'Mauriacus'. However, the terrain there is not an open plain and there are no features that conform to any descriptions of the battle.

There can be little doubt that the battle took place five Roman miles west of Troyes just as the Gallic chronicler said it did. The Battle of Campus Mauriacus, if not the Battle of Troyes, is probably the most accurate term for the encounter at the Catalaunian Fields in 451. The ridge described by Jordanes is the ridge of Montgueux and Attila was probably camped on the banks of the Seine to the north of Troyes at Saint-Lyé. Aetius followed his retreat from Orléans closely, camped overnight at the source of the Vanne and then moved into position on the heights above the modern hamlet of Grange-l'Evêque, seizing the ridge of Montgueux and offering battle on the plains below.

This is a view of the Montgueux ridge from the south from the Roman road leading to Troyes. It is much steeper on this side, and although Aetius could have skirted it here and then swung up to the north, the terrain does not accord with Jordanes' description of the battle.

THE OPENING MOVES

From Fontvannes it is just over 8km to the summit of the heights overlooking the plains to the east. The ground rises relatively gently towards the north-east before dropping off fairly sharply to the flat beyond Grange-l'Evêque. There are two good routes leading up the high ground to the left of the Montgueux ridge. These would have allowed Aetius to advance in two columns about 1km apart. Leaving at dawn, Aetius' lead elements could have been above Grange-l'Evêque by around 8 a.m. From here the Romano-Visigoths had a perfect overview of the Campus Mauriacus all the way to the Seine. Aetius and Theodoric would have been able to see Attila's camp and observe their enemy's movements.

Aetius had an alternative route open to him. He could have sent some or all of his forces directly east along the Roman road towards Troyes, skirting the Montgueux ridge to the south and then just before reaching Troyes swung north to face Attila to the west of the town. The main problem with this is that the slope of the ridge on the southern side is very steep, placing any troops he might have sent to contest the ridge at a severe disadvantage. We cannot know for certain but on balance of probabilities it is much more likely that Aetius would have chosen the route to the north-east of the ridge which gave him a relatively easy approach to the high ground and the opportunity to observe his enemy's deployment before descending to the plains to offer battle.

It is highly unlikely that Attila would have simply sat back and waited. No doubt his mobile horse archers would have been observing Aetius' movements and shadowing his approach, sending word back to Attila to give him plenty of time to deploy.

According to Jordanes the battle began with a fight to take the Montgueux ridge. He says that 'the Huns with their forces seized the right side, the Romans, the Visigoths and their allies the left, and then began a struggle for the yet untaken crest.' This is not overly helpful as right or left varies according to one's perspective. It is reasonable to assume that Jordanes would have taken Aetius' perspective rather than Attila's. If this is the case, and if Aetius did indeed advance along the two routes to the north-west of the Montgueux ridge, then to take the ridge he would have had to send the forces on his right flank to advance up the left side. This also fits with Aetius' battle deployment, which has the Visigoths on his right flank. The force which contested command of the ridge with the Huns was led by Aetius and Thorismund and therefore must have been primarily or exclusively Visigoths.

This magnificent 4th-century Roman helmet from the Danube frontier would have been worn by a leader of the highest rank. Such helmets would have been prized by Huns, Goths and others who equipped themselves from Roman arsenals. (Jebulon Muzej Vojvodine, Novi Sad)

The situation in the morning of 20 June 451. Aetius and Theodoric advance north-west along two parallel routes to seize the high ground above the modern village of Grange-l'Évêque. Thorismund engages the Hun covering force and drives them from the Montgueux ridge.

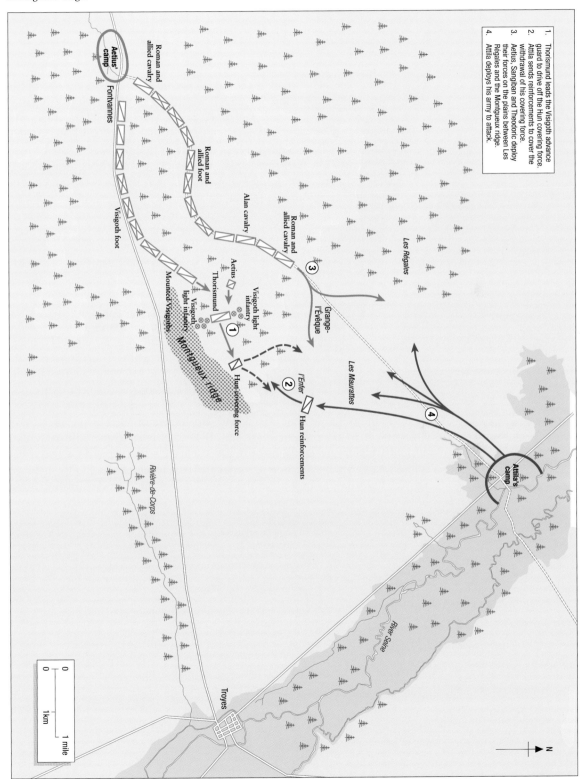

1. Thorismund leads the Visigoth advance guard to drive off the Hun covering force.
2. Attila sends reinforcements to cover the withdrawal of his covering force.
3. Aetius, Sangiban and Theodoric deploy their forces on the plains between Les Régales and the Montgueux ridge.
4. Attila deploys his army to attack.

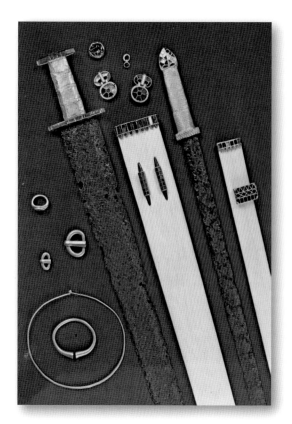

The treasure of Pouan now in the Musée Saint-Loup, Troyes. Found to the north of the battlefield in the 19th century, it was once thought that these may have been the burial goods of King Theodoric. However, it is more likely that they belonged to one of Attila's notable followers interred on the withdrawal.

Jordanes' description of the battle makes it seem as if Attila only decided to fight for the high ground as an afterthought: 'Attila sent his men to take the summit of the mountain, but was outstripped by Thorismund and Aetius, who in their effort to gain the top of the hill reached higher ground and through this advantage of position easily routed the Huns as they came up.' This is highly unlikely. The Hun covering force would have fallen back as Aetius' army moved forward. As the Romano-Visigoths passed to the north-west of the ridge, it is most likely that the Huns would have pulled back to the summit to observe their enemy's movements. Aetius would not have wanted to leave them there and so he probably tasked Thorismund with taking the summit while the rest of the army continued their march.

The fight for the ridge was clearly a prelude to the main battle. It may have been nothing more than Thorismund chasing off a small detachment of Hun scouts, although it is conceivable that Attila reinforced them. If Attila did send reinforcements to contest the ridge then it could explain Jordanes' statement that Aetius and Thorismund reached the summit first. The eastern slope is relatively steep, while the western slope is gentle. Thorismund would have had little difficulty getting to the top while any Hun reinforcements would have had to pick their way carefully along the re-entrants to gain the heights.

It is not possible that Attila had any intention of forcing a decisive engagement to take the high ground. If he had wanted to fight over hilly, difficult terrain, he could have done so closer to Orléans. His army was suited to a battle on flat, open ground and that is why he had fallen back on Troyes. If Attila did indeed send reinforcements up the ridge, his intention

could only have been to disrupt Aetius' movements, make his opponent's life more difficult and give himself more time to deploy as he wished. Despite Jordanes claim that Attila's army was 'thrown into confusion' by Thorismund's success in taking the high ground, the outcome of the fight was inevitable.

What probably happened was that Thorismund led a detachment of Visigoths from the right wing of the army to move up the left slope of the ridge and drive off the Hun covering force. Possibly Aetius accompanied him.

Most of the Visigoths would have been mounted but they may have been accompanied by some light infantry. As the Visigoths approached, the Huns would have kept their distance, probably splitting up into small groups and harassing their enemy with arrows and then withdrawing out of harm's way. The slopes of the ridge are broken up with several scrubby re-entrants. Very soon the Huns would have run out of space and been at risk to Visigoth light infantry, who could have winkled their way through dead ground and come up behind them. After a few volleys of arrows the Huns on the ridge would have had to either engage their enemy in hand-to-hand combat or pull back off the heights to rejoin their main army. If Attila did send reinforcements up the hill, it is most likely that they would have been sent to help his covering force achieve a clean break rather than a concerted effort to keep control of the summit. He wanted to fight on the flat and the battle for the ridge was merely a delaying action.

DEPLOYMENT FOR BATTLE

Assuming Aetius' vanguard had reached the high ground above the modern village of Grange-l'Evêque by about 8 a.m., the fight for the summit of Montgueux must have taken place sometime after that. Probably by 11 a.m. Thorismund would have been in command of the heights and the Hun covering force had withdrawn to rejoin their main army. Meanwhile Aetius, Sangiban and Theodoric would be leading the rest of the army down onto the plains to deploy for battle.

This is the view looking south from the centre of Aetius' line to the ridge of Montgueux.

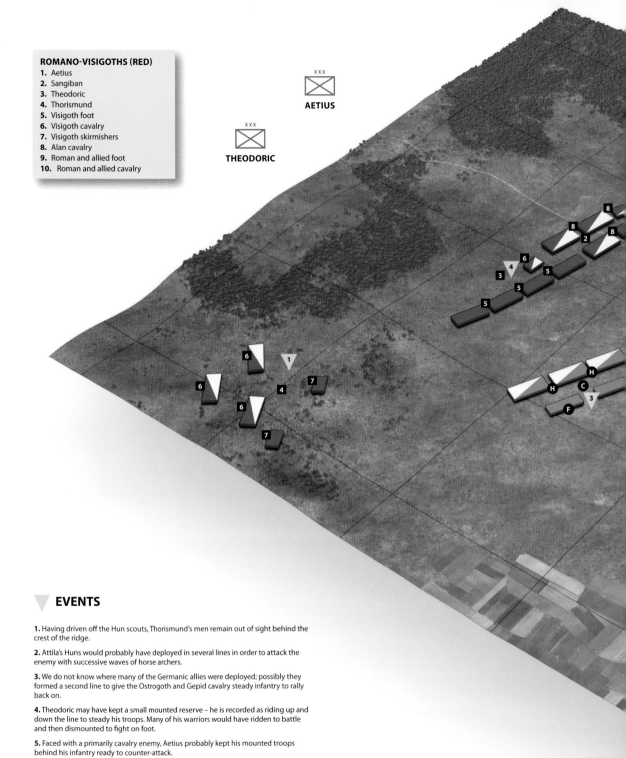

ROMANO-VISIGOTHS (RED)
1. Aetius
2. Sangiban
3. Theodoric
4. Thorismund
5. Visigoth foot
6. Visigoth cavalry
7. Visigoth skirmishers
8. Alan cavalry
9. Roman and allied foot
10. Roman and allied cavalry

AETIUS

THEODORIC

EVENTS

1. Having driven off the Hun scouts, Thorismund's men remain out of sight behind the crest of the ridge.

2. Attila's Huns would probably have deployed in several lines in order to attack the enemy with successive waves of horse archers.

3. We do not know where many of the Germanic allies were deployed; possibly they formed a second line to give the Ostrogoth and Gepid cavalry steady infantry to rally back on.

4. Theodoric may have kept a small mounted reserve – he is recorded as riding up and down the line to steady his troops. Many of his warriors would have ridden to battle and then dismounted to fight on foot.

5. Faced with a primarily cavalry enemy, Aetius probably kept his mounted troops behind his infantry ready to counter-attack.

INITIAL DEPLOYMENT, MIDDAY 20 JUNE

Following the skirmish to seize the ridge, the two armies have deployed for battle. Aetius and Theodoric have descended from the heights and adopted a defensive position to await Attila's attack. Thorismund is still on the ridge out of sight from Attila's lines.

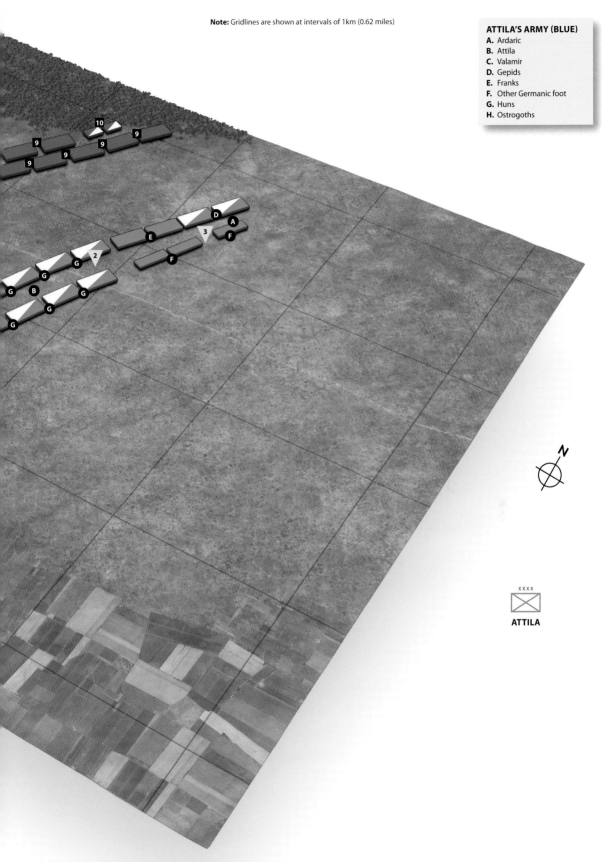

ATTILA'S ARMY (BLUE)
A. Ardaric
B. Attila
C. Valamir
D. Gepids
E. Franks
F. Other Germanic foot
G. Huns
H. Ostrogoths

xxxx
ATTILA

Aetius would have been in a stronger tactical position had he remained on the high ground rather than descending to the plains below. However, he needed a decisive battle. If he had remained on the heights, Attila could simply have refused battle and stayed in his well-supplied camp on the Seine leaving Aetius stuck on a hill with no water source. Furthermore, Aetius' unlikely conglomeration of allies would have begun to drift away if the campaign became bogged down into a war of attrition. The position Aetius chose was, therefore, strong but not so strong as to tempt Attila to refuse or delay battle.

One of the greatest problems facing a mobile horse-archer enemy is protecting the flanks and rear of the army. If Aetius had advanced out into the middle of the plain then Attila's more numerous and more mobile cavalry could have encircled him. Therefore it is probable that Aetius deployed with his right flank protected by the ridge of Montgueux, now occupied by Thorismund's Visigoths. To his rear was the high ground he had just passed over and a wooded spur, known today as Les Régales, extended out into the plains to effectively protect his left flank. There was no practical way for Attila to get around his flanks or rear and if things went badly Aetius could withdraw back up onto the high ground where pursuit would be more difficult.

Theodoric and the Visigoths held the right wing. Although many of them would have ridden into battle, it is quite likely that most or all would have dismounted to form a shieldwall in order to be less vulnerable to Hun archery. Thorismund's contingent probably remained on the heights of the Montgueux ridge, still mounted in order to be able to quickly move down and influence the battle at a critical moment. Looking up from the plains below it is possible to see the edge of the crest, but the slope of the ridge is such that any troops just a few metres back cannot be seen. Once he had lost the fight for the hill, Attila could not have known whether or not some enemy were still there.

Aetius placed Sangiban's Alans in the centre, 'thus contriving with military caution to surround by a host of faithful troops the man in whose loyalty they had little confidence. For one who has difficulties placed in the way of his flight readily submits to the necessity of fighting' (Jordanes). The left wing was held by the Romans, presumably also including the other smaller

This silvered helmet now in the Germanisches Nationalmuseu, Nuremberg, is a fine example of what is thought to be a typical late Roman infantry helmet. It is characterised by a two-part bowl held together by a central ridge, often with a metal or horsehair plume attached. The original would have had cheek guards. The nose guard is relatively unusual for this helmet style. (Wolfgang Sauber)

contingents such as the Franks, Burgundians, Saxons and Armoricans. We have no details as to how they were deployed but probably, like the Visigoths, the majority formed a shieldwall supported by foot archers, perhaps with a mounted contingent held back in reserve ready to intervene in case the enemy broke through or to exploit success.

Attila had plenty of time to move out from his camp and marshal his forces while his covering force was delaying Aetius on the heights of Montgueux. He had never been defeated in battle and he was in a position of his own choosing, even if Aetius' deployment dictated a frontal assault. His army was rested and well supplied, thanks to the Bishop of Troyes, and he should have been feeling quite confident.

Jordanes, however, paints a very different picture:

Then Attila, king of the Huns, was taken aback by [the retreat from Orléans] and lost confidence in his own troops, so that he feared to begin the conflict. While he was meditating on flight; a greater calamity than death itself; he decided to inquire into the future through soothsayers. So, as was their custom, they examined the entrails of cattle and certain streaks in bones that had been scraped, and foretold disaster to the Huns. Yet as a slight consolation they prophesied that the chief commander of the foe they were to meet should fall and mar by his death the rest of the victory and the triumph. Now Attila deemed the death of Aetius a thing to be desired even at the cost of his own life, for Aetius stood in the way of his plans. So although he was disturbed by this prophecy, yet inasmuch as he was a man who sought counsel of omens in all warfare, he began the battle with anxious heart.

The area at the foot of the Montgueux ridge is marked on modern French maps as 'l'Enfer' or 'hell'. This is the slope where Thorismund's Goths would have charged down onto the left flank of Attila's line.

Writing after the event much of this is probably hindsight on Jordanes' part laced with a fair amount of dramatic licence. He would have been in no position to understand Attila's mind. It may be true that the king of the Huns had not counted on an alliance between Aetius and Theodoric nor on being rebuffed from the gates of Orléans, but Attila had no reason to suppose that he might lose the battle on the Mauriacian Plains outside Troyes. As it turned out it was Theodoric who fell in battle not Aetius, but again the whole passage was written well after the events were known.

Jordanes goes on to describe Attila's deployment:

> The battle line of the Huns was arranged so that Attila and his bravest followers were stationed in the centre. In arranging them thus the king had chiefly his own safety in view, since by his position in the very midst of his race he would be kept out of the way of threatening danger. The innumerable peoples of the divers tribes, which he had subjected to his sway, formed the wings.

The Ostrogoths held Attila's left wing and the Gepids the right. We have no idea how the other minor contingents were arrayed. 'Now the rest of the crowd of kings (if we may call them so) and the leaders of various nations hung upon Attila's nod like slaves, and when he gave a sign even by a glance, without a murmur each stood forth in fear and trembling and did as he was bid.'

The Franks, Burgundians, Thuringians, Alamanni, Rugians, Heruls and other smaller contingents were possibly split between the Ostrogoth and Gepid wings but if so we have no indication in what proportion nor on which wing they may have been stationed. None of our sources make any mention of their parts in the battle. Probably the vast majority of Attila's allies would have been mounted and some of the German contingents who traditionally fought on foot may have formed a second line for the cavalry to rally back on.

The view from the left of Attila's line looking towards the position where Theodoric's Visigoths would have been stationed. The ridge of Montgueux is on the left, where Thorismund's men could have easily been concealed.

Jordanes claims that Attila's army was thrown into confusion by losing the fight for command of the heights of Montgueux. As a result Attila felt the need to give a speech of encouragement to his troops before the general engagement began. As with much of Jordanes' account we should not take this too literally but it does indicate that the battle for the hill was a prelude to the main action. The speech, of course, is a dramatic device but the words Jordanes invented (or copied from another source) do give some indication of the tactical considerations and possible attitudes:

Here you stand, after conquering mighty nations and subduing the world. I therefore think it foolish for me to goad you with words, as though you were men who had not been proved in action. Let a new leader or an untried army resort to that. It is not right for me to say anything common, nor ought you to listen. For what is war but your usual custom? Or what is sweeter for a brave man than to seek revenge with his own hand? It is a right of nature to glut the soul with vengeance. Let us then attack the foe eagerly; for they are ever the bolder who make the attack. Despise this union of discordant races! To defend oneself by alliance is proof of cowardice.

See, even before our attack they are smitten with terror. They seek the heights, they seize the hills and, repenting too late, clamour for protection against battle in the open fields. You know how slight a matter the Roman attack is. While they are still gathering in order and forming in one line with locked shields, they are checked, I will not say by the first wound, but even by the dust of battle.

Then on to the fray with stout hearts, as is your wont. Despise their battle line. Attack the Alans, smite the Visigoths! Seek swift victory in that spot where the battle rages. For when the sinews are cut the limbs soon relax, nor can a body stand when you have taken away the bones. Let your courage rise and your own fury burst forth! Now show your cunning, Huns, now your deeds of arms! Let the wounded exact in return the death of his foe; let the unwounded revel in slaughter of the enemy.

This is the view from the centre of Attila's lines looking towards the modern village of Grange l'Évêque. Nestled into the high ground behind him, Aetius' right flank was protected by the Montgueux ridge, and his left by the wooded high ground now known as Les Regales.

No spear shall harm those who are sure to live; and those who are sure to die. Fate overtakes even in peace. And finally, why should Fortune have made the Huns victorious over so many nations, unless it were to prepare them for the joy of this conflict … Even a mass of federated nations could not endure the sight of the Huns. I am not deceived in the issue: here is the field so many victories have promised us. I shall hurl the first spear at the foe. If any can stand at rest while Attila fights, he is a dead man.

It is interesting that the words Jordanes puts into Attila's mouth emphasise the locked shields of the Romano-Visigoth line and the defensive position they adopted. He also stresses the point that Aetius and Theodoric kept to the heights rather than advancing all the way out into the open plains. It is not much to go on but it does seem to confirm Aetius' deployment being tucked into the hills and probably centred on the modern village of Grange-l'Evêque with the ridge of Montgueux protecting his right and Les Régales protecting his left. Aetius may have taken the strategic initiative by forcing Attila back from Orléans but once in position he set up a defensive array, enticing Attila to attack him.

THE CLASH OF BATTLE LINES

Unfortunately the details we have of the actual combat are very sketchy. Again we have to depend almost exclusively on Jordanes. His account only describes the action on the Visigoth wing and almost completely ignores everyone else. Therefore any reconstruction must fall back on conjecture based on what we know about the fighting methods of the troops involved.

From the top to the Montgueux ridge Thorismund would have had this clear view of the plains below. It would have been relatively easy for him to remain concealed behind the crest of the ridge until the opportune moment to charge into the left flank of Attila's army.

Although Jordanes says that Attila positioned himself in the middle of his battle array due to safety considerations, it is far more likely that this was done with the intent of breaking through in the centre. Due to the high, rough ground on both flanks he could not hope to envelop his enemy. He would have seen that Aetius had put his weakest troops, the Alans, in the centre and had time to readjust his deployment to take advantage of this. He probably hoped that the Ostrogoths on the left and the Gepids on the right would be able to pin the Visigoths and Romans respectively, giving the Huns time to break the Alans, separate the two main enemy contingents and then turn out on them.

The Alan contingent was relatively small so the Huns in the centre would have overlapped the opposing Roman and Visigoth wings. This would have allowed Attila to support the Ostrogoth and Gepid attacks with his horse archers, weakening and disrupting the enemy line and making it more vulnerable to a charge. It is rare for a mounted charge to succeed against determined infantry. If, however, the latter are weakened by archery, causing the integrity of the line to break up, then a frontal cavalry charge can possibly succeed.

The Huns would have attacked in a succession of wedge-shaped bands to maximise the effect of their archery. Ammianus says that 'they purposely divide suddenly into scattered bands and attack, rushing about in disorder here and there, dealing terrific slaughter.' This is maybe what it seemed like to a Roman observer but effective horse-archer tactics would have required a great deal of training, teamwork, coordination and control. What Ammianus calls 'rushing about in disorder' would have been anything but that. Each man would have to keep his place, maintain sufficient spacing to allow for turns and follow closely the signals given by the horsetail standard of his leader.

Lajos Kassai's modern horse-archery experiments have shown how it is possible to cover a 90m course in under seven seconds, firing three accurate arrows in the process. Each horse archer holds a bunch of arrows in his left hand against his bow and fires in rapid succession. The first shots are on the ride towards the enemy, the next as the unit splits right and left, shooting to the side, and the final 'Parthian shot' to the rear as the men gallop back towards their own lines.

The physical and psychological impact on the Romans and Visigoths cowering behind their shields must have been immense. The initial wedge formation would have concentrated a storm of arrows on a relatively narrow front. The men who suffered this would then have to stand firm as a fierce-looking bunch of men galloped towards them with ill intent. Then suddenly the Huns would break right and left and wheel back towards their own lines loosing two more arrow storms in the process. Giving the target no respite, a second line would be advancing forward in the same way while the first line peeled back. The Huns could keep this up for hours, attacking in successive waves until gaps began to appear in the shield wall and an opportunity was presented for hand-to-hand combat.

The Romans and Visigoths would have been supported by archers firing over the heads of the spearmen and most of the spearmen also had javelins or darts. Even though the volume of missiles would have been nothing like what the Huns could deliver, they were not entirely hapless victims. Protected by large oval shields the impact of the Huns' charges would have been mostly

THE HUN ATTACK (PP. 70–71)

In wedge formation the Huns have loosed an arrow storm against the defending Romans, and now the lead men break right and left to ride along the Roman front shooting more arrows at close range. They will keep this up with a succession of charges until the enemy shieldwall begins to waver, at which point they will close in with spears and swords. The psychological impact of the charging horsemen and arrow storm would have been immense, but protected by their large oval shields the Romans will only suffer a few casualties as long as they hold their nerve.

Seeing the rear ranks beginning to waver, the Roman officer (1) is encouraging his men, reminding them that as long as they hold their formation they will be able to withstand the Huns. His shield pattern identifies the unit as the Batavi luniores. We do not know which units were present at the battle but this unit is listed in the *Notitia Dignitatum* as part of the Gallic field army in the early 5th century.

Armed with light javelins and darts in addition to their spears, the Roman infantry (2) are able to give some response to the Huns even when it does not come to close combat. The darts, called *martiobarbuli,* are held in a clip behind the shields. No doubt there would be a rank of archers behind the heavy infantry who would be firing overhead.

The Huns (3) are well armed with Roman armour and weapons supplementing their native equipment. The formidable composite bow, however, remains their primary weapon and the addition of Roman armour is no impediment to their mobility. Several men have spears slung from their backs and lassos from their saddles, which they would use when it came to close combat.

psychological. As long as the shieldwall held its nerve, with men from the rear ranks moving up to replace casualties, they could endure. This seems to be what happened.

> Hand to hand they clashed in battle, and the fight grew fierce, confused, monstrous, unrelenting – a fight whose like no ancient time has ever recorded. There such deeds were done that a brave man who missed this marvellous spectacle could not hope to see anything so wonderful all his life long. For, if we may believe our elders, a brook flowing between low banks through the plain was greatly increased by blood from the wounds of the slain. It was not flooded by showers, as brooks usually rise, but was swollen by a strange stream and turned into a torrent by the increase of blood. Those whose wounds drove them to slake their parching thirst drank water mingled with gore. In their wretched plight they were forced to drink what they thought was the blood they had poured from their own wounds. (Jordanes)

The fight in the centre would have been slightly different. The Alans had no tradition of fighting on foot and many of them would have been armed and equipped in a similar manner to the Huns. Rather than presenting a solid shieldwall, the Alan horse archers would have responded in kind, exchanging arrows with the Huns with bands from both sides becoming intermingled as they rode through and around each other. The Alans, however, were not entirely devoted to Aetius' cause and it seems as though the Huns had the better of them. Jordanes says that the Visigoths became separated from the Alans, probably as the latter began to fall back.

This is the position at the extreme left of Attila's line. Just behind the crest of the ridge Thorismund's Visigoths would have been waiting for the opportune moment to crash into the left flank of Attila's army.

ROMANO-VISIGOTHS (RED)
1. Aetius
2. Sangiban
3. Theodoric
4. Thorismund
5. Visigoth foot
6. Visigoth cavalry
7. Visigoth skirmishers
8. Alan cavalry
9. Roman and allied foot
10. Roman and allied cavalry

AETIUS

THEODORIC

▼ **EVENTS**

1. Sangiban's Alans are driven back by the Huns in the centre.

2. The Huns turn in on the flanks of the Romans and Visigoths. King Theodoric is killed when he rides up to rally his men as the Visigoth line begins to waiver.

3. Roman and allied cavalry reserves move up to plug the gap created by the retreating Alans.

4. Thorismund leads his men down the ridge and into the flank of the Ostrogoths.

5. The Roman and allied foot manage to hold successive charges by Ardaric's Germanic warriors.

THE TURNING POINT, LATE AFTERNOON 20 JUNE

The Huns have broken through in the centre, driving the Alans back and separating the Visigoth and Roman wings. King Theodoric is killed as he rallies his men and at this critical moment Thorismund charges down the ridge into the enemy flank.

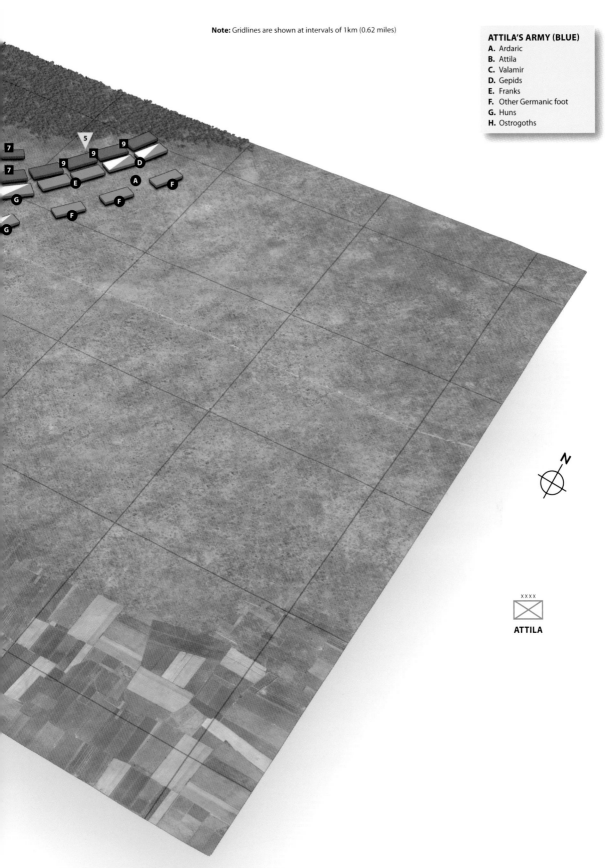

Note: Gridlines are shown at intervals of 1km (0.62 miles)

ATTILA'S ARMY (BLUE)
A. Ardaric
B. Attila
C. Valamir
D. Gepids
E. Franks
F. Other Germanic foot
G. Huns
H. Ostrogoths

N

xxxx
ATTILA

The left flank of the Visigoths suffered from Hun archery and was in danger of being outflanked as the Alans retired. Meanwhile, the main part of their line had to face a succession of charges from their Ostrogoth cousins. Here shock action rather than archery would have been the order of the day. Armed with lances and javelins the Ostrogoths would have ridden towards the Visigoth line, hoping to break it by sheer force. If the men in the shieldwall held their nerve, presenting an unbroken line of spears and shields and closing any gaps as soon as they appeared, the horsemen would have been unable to break through. They may have exchanged a few blows with the front ranks of the infantry but then would have been forced to wheel back and rally for a second charge.

Presumably (because we have no source which gives any information of the action on that wing), a similar situation was occurring on Aetius' left wing where the Romans, Franks, Burgundians, Saxons and Armoricans faced Ardaric's Gepids and others. Here some of the combat may have been between infantry forces as many of Attila's other Germanic allies preferred to fight on foot.

A clash of two opposing infantry formations would have been more deliberate than the mounted actions. As Attila's Germanic foot advanced on Aetius' Romans and Germans, both sides would try to intimidate the other by clashing their spears on their shields and raising the *barritus* war cry: 'a shout which they raise when a fight is actually at boiling point; it begins with a low murmur and gradually increases in volume until it resounds like the sea dashing against a cliff' (Ammianus Marcellinus).

The view from Mont Aimé to the south-west of modern Châlons. There is a remote possibility that the battle could have taken place here as there is high ground dominating a plain. However, to reach Châlons Attila would have had to give up a far more favourable battlefield at Troyes.

Arrows from the rear of the Roman ranks would have rained down on the heads of their enemies as they came into range and then, as the lines closed, a more deadly exchange of missiles would have occurred. Franks would have hurled their *franciscae* (throwing axes) and angons (heavy javelins) while the Romans would have unleashed a volley of javelins and light darts. Then the lines would have clashed in close combat; the men in the front ranks thrusting their shields into the faces of their enemy while seeking an opportunity to stab with swords and spears. Meanwhile the rear ranks would continue to shower their opponents with javelins and arrows. The combat would have swayed back and forth in a deadly, drawn-out scrum.

We do not know what was happening on Aetius' left but it is clear that the Visigoths on the right were under immense pressure. King Theodoric rode up and down the line to steady his men and keep the shieldwall intact as they faced the Ostrogoths while the Huns began to threaten their left flank. As he was doing so, disaster struck:

> While riding by to encourage his army, Theodoric was thrown from his horse and trampled under foot by his own men, thus ending his days at a ripe old age. But others say he was slain by the spear of Andag of the host of the Ostrogoths. (Jordanes)

However Theodoric's life ended, his death might easily have caused his followers to break. They had been under terrible pressure. Nerves would have been strained almost beyond human endurance and the death of their king could have ended it. Assuming the Alans had already pulled back from the line, if the Visigoths then broke, it would have been all over for Aetius.

At that moment, however, Thorismund intervened to save the day.

TURNING THE TIDE

Jordanes tells us that, after being separated from the Alans and after the death of Theodoric, the Visigoths 'fell upon the horde of the Huns and nearly slew Attila. But he prudently took flight and straightway shut himself and his companions within the barriers of the camp, which he had fortified with wagons'.

Jordanes does not say who led this Visigoth charge but it could only have been Thorismund. If the shieldwall of men on foot surged forward after their enemies to avenge their king, the line would have broken up and the mounted Huns and Ostrogoths would have been able to cut through them with relative ease just like the Normans did to Harold's men at Hastings.

In the following passage Jordanes adds: 'Thorismund, the son of King Theodoric, who with Aetius had seized the hill and repulsed the enemy from the higher ground, came unwittingly to the wagons of the enemy in the darkness of night.' This could confirm that it was Thorismund who led the charge and then the pursuit. Rather bizarrely Jordanes says that as he reached Attila's wagons, Thorismund thought he was back at his own lines. Unless he had a most unfortunate sense of direction, it is scarcely believable that Thorismund could have mistaken a ride of several kilometres over flat ground towards the Seine for pulling back towards the high ground over which he had marched earlier in the day.

THE VISIGOTHS PREPARE TO CHARGE (PP. 78–79)

After chasing the Huns off the high ground dominating the plain below, Thorismund's Visigoths have held back out of sight behind the crest of the ridge. Now that Attila's army has become decisively engaged, Thorismund gathers his men to charge down onto the enemy flank.

Having ridden out in front of his men, Thorismund **(1)** gives the signal to begin the attack. His shield pattern and clothing colours are conjectural but green and red were apparently a favoured Gothic colour combination. The entwined serpents on his shield are similar to designs carried by Germanic cavalry serving in the Roman army.

The Gothic cavalrymen **(2)** would have been born within the Roman Empire and had had access to Roman arms and expertise for several generations. They are thus very well equipped. Primarily armed with spears, they also have good swords and several of them have light javelins in a case slung from the horns of their saddles. They and Thorismund are clean shaven, as was the Visigoth fashion at the time.

On the plains below, the left flank of Attila's army **(3)** is composed of Ostrogoths and other Germans. They will bear the brunt of Thorismund's initial charge. In the centre of the battlefield the Huns, attacking in a succession of wedge-shaped formations **(4)**, are making headway against Sangiban's Alans and threatening the flanks of the Visigoths and Romans on either side. In the far distance, about 7km behind the lines, Attila's camp is spread out along the banks of the Seine **(5)**.

From the Hun lines, looking up towards the ridge of Montgueux, it is impossible to see anything beyond the crest. It would have been perfectly easy for Thorismund to remain concealed with a fairly large body of men and wait for the right moment to charge down onto the flank of his enemies while they were engaged against his father and brother's shieldwall. The flat ground at the foot of the ridge to the north-west is known today as 'l'Enfer' or 'hell'. This place would have been at the extreme left of Attila's line and it is aptly named if it was here that Thorismund charged into the enemy flank.

If the main engagement started some time in the early afternoon and Thorismund's pursuit brought him to the Hun camp after darkness in mid-summer, a great deal must have happened that is not fully explained by Jordanes' short description. It is unlikely Thorismund would have held back out of the battle for hours. Most probably he would have waited for the initial feints and skirmishes to end, timing his intervention to coincide with the lines becoming decisively engaged. From the top of the ridge, concealed in cover, Thorismund could easily have observed the entire battlefield below. Possibly he saw his father fall and that may have spurred him into the attack. On the other hand, as Jordanes' chronology is far from clear, Thorismund's intervention may have been much earlier.

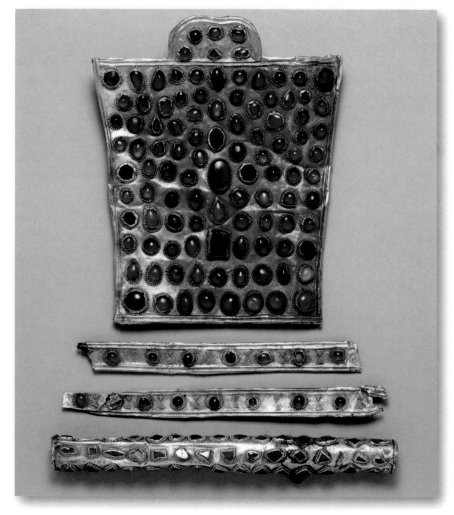

These Hun horse trappings found in south-western Russia are of gold, decorated with gemstones. The large piece is an ornamental chamfron, the two thin strips are bridle mounts and the tube is the handle of a riding whip. (Walters Art Museum)

It is more than likely that Thorismund's men remained mounted. The slope of the ridge descends relatively gently to the plains below on the north-eastern side. It would have given momentum to men charging down it without making such a move too difficult or disruptive even if on horseback. As Thorismund later led the pursuit as far as the Hun wagon laager, around 7km to the east, he must have been mounted to have been able to do so.

A surprise mounted charge into the flank of enemy engaged to their front would have had a devastating impact. Jordanes implies that it was then all over rather quickly, with the Huns retreating immediately to the safety of their fortified camp. Rather surprisingly Jordanes does not mention the Ostrogoths again after their possible role in killing King Theodoric. Surely it would have been the Ostrogoths on the left of the line who would have felt the initial impact of Thorismund's charge and who would have been the first to break. As a Gothic propagandist it was, however, Jordanes' job to glorify the deeds of the Goths on both sides and so it is perhaps not so strange that he does not say anything about the Ostrogoths being defeated. Far better to have the Visigoths fall on the Huns and to speak only of the Huns in the context of defeat.

If it is unlikely that Thorismund remained on the hill for hours, and if it is true what Jordanes says about pursuit carrying on until after dark then the retreat of Attila's army must have been a gradual withdrawal rather than an instant rout. The combat seems to have become very confused with the battle lines breaking up and bands of men becoming separated from their comrades and intermingled with those of the enemy.

'Aetius also became separated from his men in the confusion of night and wandered about in the midst of the enemy. Fearing disaster had happened, he went about in search of the Goths. At last he reached the camp of his allies and passed the remainder of the night in the protection of their shields.' This passage from Jordanes gives some indication of just how confused the battle had become. If it is true that Aetius ended up in the Visigoth lines at nightfall then it may indicate that the left wing also had success against the Gepids, freeing him up to lead the Roman cavalry reserve in pursuit, joining up with Thorismund in the centre.

Opposite Mont Aimé there is a steep ridge, which could possibly be the ridge that Jordanes tells of. However, the slope is very steep and would not be conducive to a mounted charge into the flank of Attila's line.

It is quite impossible to reconstruct the final stages of the battle. Probably Thorismund's charge was decisive and turned the tide against Attila but we cannot know this for certain. Possibly the Romans succeeded in holding against Ardaric's wing and some of them, led by Aetius, were freed to turn their attention against the Huns in the centre. If the Huns had moved into the gap created by the retreating Alans then they were in danger of being cut off and surrounded as their enemies moved in on the wings. A retreat, therefore, was Attila's only option.

The fighting raged on over the entire plains as the Huns fell back to their wagon laager. Some bands of horse archers would have covered the retreat, holding up the pursuers then withdrawing behind their supports who in turn would cover their move. They had plenty of space to do this as the ground was flat and open for 7km to the rear and many more in both directions to the flanks. Evidence for an orderly withdrawal rather than a rout is hinted at in Jordanes' description of intense combat right up to the Hun wagons: 'As [Thorismund] was fighting bravely, someone wounded him in the head and dragged him from his horse. Then he was rescued by the watchful care of his followers and withdrew from the fierce conflict.'

This 4th-century painting shows a late Roman soldier wearing wrist-length mail, a metal crested helmet and carrying two javelins behind a round or oval shield.

Full darkness, which would have come after 10 p.m. on 20 June, put an end to the fighting. Attila was defeated but his army was not destroyed. 'Attila shut himself and his companions within the barriers of the camp, which he had fortified with wagons. A frail defence indeed; yet there they sought refuge for their lives, whom but a little while before no walls of earth could withstand' (Jordanes). The Romans and Visigoths camped on the field, apparently quite close to the Huns as on the following day we learn that a shower of arrows from the Roman camp was able to keep the Huns at bay.

This is the view from the centre of Aetius' line. The high ground in the distance is to the east of the Seine, where Attila had his camp.

ROMANO-VISIGOTHS (RED)
1. Aetius
2. Thorismund
3. Roman and allied cavalry
4. Visigoth mounted warriors
5. Visigoth foot warriors
6. Roman and allied infantry

XXX
AETIUS

XXX
THORISMUND

▼ **EVENTS**

1. Hun horse archers closest to the enemy fall back behind supports, shooting as they withdraw.

2. German warriors on foot may have provided stable points for the horse archers to move through.

3. Many of the Visigoths who fought on foot during the battle would have mounted up to join in the pursuit.

4. A second line of horse archers moves up to inflict further delay on the pursuers.

5. Having made a clean break from the enemy individual groups of men make their own way back to the camp.

6. Romans and Visigoths on foot follow up behind the cavalry.

THE PURSUIT, EVENING 20 JUNE

Attila's left flank crumbles and he orders a retreat back to his camp. It is a fighting withdrawal rather than a rout, and fierce combat continues until darkness puts an end to it.

Note: Gridlines are shown at intervals of 1km (0.62 miles)

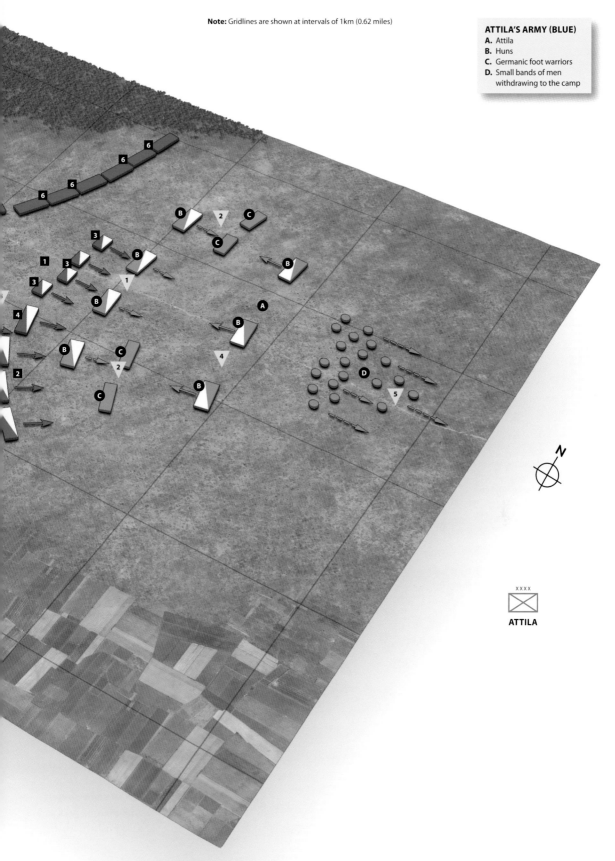

ATTILA'S ARMY (BLUE)
A. Attila
B. Huns
C. Germanic foot warriors
D. Small bands of men
    withdrawing to the camp

N

XXXX
ATTILA

THE DAY AFTER

> At dawn on the following day, when the Romans saw the fields were piled high with bodies and that the Huns did not venture forth, they thought the victory was theirs, but knew that Attila would not flee from the battle unless overwhelmed by a great disaster. Yet he did nothing cowardly, like one that is overcome, but with clash of arms sounded the trumpets and threatened an attack. He was like a lion pierced by hunting spears, who paces to and fro before the mouth of his den and dares not spring, but ceases not to terrify the neighbourhood by his roaring. Even so this warlike king at bay terrified his conquerors. (Jordanes)

The victorious allied leaders got together to discuss what to do next and decided to lay siege to Attila's camp. Although the camp was well sited, it was now cut off from supplies while Aetius' army would have been able to re-provision from Troyes and the surrounding countryside.

'It was said that [Attila] remained supremely brave even in this extremity and had heaped up a funeral pyre of horse trappings, so that if the enemy should attack him, he was determined to cast himself into the flames, that none might have the joy of wounding him and that the lord of so many races might not fall into the hands of his foes' (Jordanes). Hun saddles were made of wood, like those still used by their descendants in central Asia today, so a pyre of horse furniture would have been feasible.

But it did not come to this. The Visigoths recovered the body of their fallen king and 'bore forth the royal majesty with sounding arms, and valiant Thorismund, as befitted a son, honoured the glorious spirit of his dear father by following his remains' (Jordanes). After this Thorismund was eager to avenge his father and proposed an assault on the Hun camp. Aetius dissuaded him in what has become one of the many mysteries of the battle.

Having Attila at his mercy, surely it would be logical for Aetius to finish the job and destroy his enemy completely. However, Aetius had been a friend of the Huns and an enemy of the Visigoths for many years. Quite possibly Aetius hoped that by not destroying the Huns they could continue to provide a useful balance of power to the Visigoths. This is certainly what Jordanes thought:

A silver dish depicting the Emperor Valentinian I with guardsmen wearing helmets with tall feathered plumes. The shield designs are very similar to those shown in the *Notitia Dignitatum*.

> Aetius feared that if the Huns were totally destroyed by the Goths, the Roman Empire would be overwhelmed, and urgently advised [Thorismund] to return to his own dominions to take up the rule which his father had left. Otherwise his brothers might seize their father's possessions and obtain the power over the Visigoths. In this case Thorismund would have to fight fiercely and, what is worse, disastrously with his

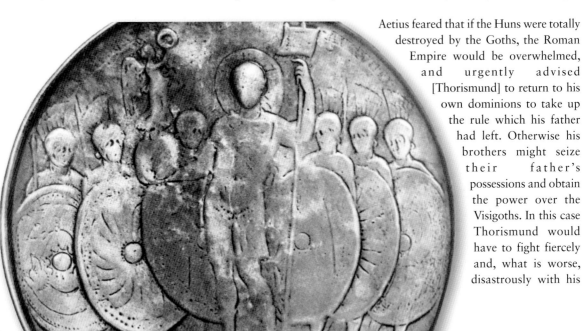

This is the view from Attila's line looking towards the centre of Aetius' position.

own countrymen. Thorismund accepted the advice without perceiving its double meaning, but followed it with an eye toward his own advantage. So he left the Huns and returned to Gaul. Thus while human frailty rushes into suspicion, it often loses an opportunity of doing great things. (Jordanes)

Gregory of Tours says much the same happened with Aetius' Frankish allies:

> When the battle was finished, Aetius said to Thorismund: 'Make haste and return swiftly to your native land, for fear you lose your father's kingdom because of your brother.' The latter, on hearing this, departed speedily with the intention of anticipating his brother, and seizing his father's throne first. At the same time Aetius, by a stratagem, caused the king of the Franks to flee. When they had gone, Aetius took the spoils of the battle and returned victoriously to his country with much booty.

These stories may or may not be true. Thorismund's position was precarious as later history proved: he was killed by his younger brother Theodoric II, who in turn was assassinated later by another brother Eurich. So the heir apparent had every reason to depart the field quickly and get back to Toulouse to secure his throne. It is even possible that the Goths and Franks departed against Aetius' wishes and the above stories were invented to add greater nobility to their tales.

Most warriors on both sides would have worn spangenhelm-style helmets like this gilded example from Krefeld-Gellep. There are indications that it probably had a mail neck guard. Probably the rank and file would have had to make do with less elaborate versions.

There is, however, one other version of events recounted in the *Chronicle of Fredegar* (a 7th-century history of the Franks). Here we are told that Aetius promised the Huns and Goths half of Gaul each for defending it against the other. Then he extorted 10,000 gold solidi from both of them. Fredegar asserts that, rather than letting the Huns go, Aetius with Romans and Franks pursued them into Thuringia.

Whatever the truth of the matter, Attila seems to have been able to withdraw from the field in relatively good order and make it back across the Rhine to his heartland in Pannonia.

AFTERMATH

So was the Catalaunian Fields really one of the decisive battles of the Western world? As befitting their era, 18th- and 19th-century historians tended to see it as the last stand of empire and a triumph of Christendom over rampaging barbarous heathens. In *The Fifteen Decisive Battles of the World* (1851) Sir Edward Creasy wrote: 'the battle not only rescued for a time from destruction the old age of Rome, but preserved for centuries of power and glory the Germanic element in the civilisation of modern Europe.'

In a more cynical age modern writers tend to downplay it. Typical of this view is J. B. Bury's assessment: 'The Battle of Maurica was a battle of nations, but its significance has been enormously exaggerated in conventional history. It cannot in any reasonable sense be designated as one of the critical battles of the world … The danger did not mean so much as has been commonly assumed. If Attila had been victorious … there is no reason to suppose that the course of history would have been seriously altered.'

These magnificent grave goods now in the Burg Lin Museum, Krefeld, are the panoply of a wealthy Frankish chieftain. Although the Franks are famed for fighting primarily on foot, the treasure includes gold and garnet horse furniture.

88

The truth probably lies somewhere between these two extremes. We cannot know what might have happened had Attila won. Quite possibly much would have been destroyed which ended up being preserved. Equally possibly Attila may have come to some arrangement with Ravenna and established a kingdom for himself within the Western Empire. Had this been the case, he may well have settled down to rule it in much the same way as the Franks did after their later conquest of Gaul. The Huns, however, had far less respect for Graeco-Roman civilisation than most of the other barbarian invaders and had they been able to carve out a kingdom in France then the course of European history surely would have changed significantly.

Aetius' achievement was considerable. If nothing else his success after being dealt a very poor hand is a tribute to his leadership, diplomatic, strategic and tactical skills. As such he deserves to be remembered as one of the greatest leaders of late antiquity. However admirable his achievement, the truth of the matter was that Attila suffered a setback but was not entirely defeated.

Many historians have criticised Aetius for not destroying Attila's army when he had the chance. After taking heavy casualties, and facing an inevitable break-up of the temporary alliance, he probably had no choice. Even if he was not motivated by a strategic desire to keep the Huns as a counterbalance to the rising Visigoth power, he was probably wise to give his enemy a line of retreat rather than force another costly engagement.

Attila may have lost the opportunity to carve out a kingdom in Gaul but his power was still immense and his ambition not yet curbed. The following year he invaded Italy, sacked Aquileia, Milan and Pavia, then laid waste to the countryside around. One of the consequences of this was the founding of Venice by people fleeing the Huns and seeking refuge in the marshes and

When he realised that victory was no longer possible, Attila withdrew his forces to his fortified camp on the backs of the Seine. Here his rear would have been secured by the fast flowing river, giving his army ample water, while his front and flanks would have been protected by a barricade of wagons.

lagoons. According to Priscus, Attila wanted to march on Rome but was persuaded against it to avoid tempting fate. Alaric the Goth had sacked Rome in 410 and died very shortly afterwards. The superstitious Attila apparently did not want the same thing happening to him.

Having amassed no small amount of loot, Attila withdrew from Italy later in the year. Why he did so is not clear. Much of the credit is given to Pope Leo who travelled with an embassy from the emperor Valentinian and met Attila at his camp on the shores of Lake Garda. As Jordanes relates: 'Then Attila quickly put aside his usual fury, turned back on the way he had advanced from beyond the Danube and departed with the promise of peace. But above all he declared and avowed with threats that he would bring worse things upon Italy, unless they sent him Honoria, the sister of the emperor Valentinian and daughter of Augusta Placidia, with her due share of the royal wealth.'

Another more prosaic explanation is that Attila's army was suffering from plague and famine while the Eastern emperor Marcian had sent troops to help the West. According to the *Chronicle of Hydatius*: 'The Huns, who had been plundering Italy and who had also stormed a number of cities, were victims of divine punishment, being visited with heaven-sent disasters: famine and some kind of disaster. In addition, they were slaughtered by auxiliaries sent by the Emperor Marcian and led by Aetius [confusingly, an East Roman of the same name, not the victor of the Catalaunian Fields]'.

Clearly matters were not settled and although Attila left Italy, he did so with a promise to return if his demands were not met. What finally put an end to the Hun threat was the death of the great man himself the following year.

According to Jordanes, quoting Priscus, this happened at a feast to celebrate his marriage to a new wife called Ildico:

> [Attila] had given himself up to excessive joy at his wedding, and as he lay on his back, heavy with wine and sleep, a rush of superfluous blood, which would ordinarily have flowed from his nose, streamed in deadly course down his throat and killed him, since it was hindered in the usual passages. Thus did drunkenness put a disgraceful end to a king renowned in war. On the following day, when a great part of the morning was spent, the royal attendants suspected some ill and, after a great uproar, broke in the doors. There they found the death of Attila accomplished by an effusion of blood, without any wound, and the girl with downcast face weeping beneath her veil.

This story may or may not be true. Some historians have postulated that this death was a deliberate assassination, possibly instigated by the Eastern emperor or possibly by the Burgundians as revenge for their defeat by the Huns in 437. In the latter version, recounted in Norse sagas, Attila was killed by his wife Gudrun. In any case the Hun empire fell apart after Attila's death. His sons vied for control and the Germanic subjects rose in revolt. Led by Ardaric, Attila's right-hand man at the Catalaunian Fields, the Gepids and many other German tribes defeated the Huns at the Battle of Nedao in Pannonia in 454:

> There an encounter took place between the various nations Attila had held under his sway ... Being deprived of their head, they madly strove against each other. They never found their equals ranged against them without harming

each other by wounds mutually given. And so the bravest nations tore themselves to pieces. For then, I think, must have occurred a most remarkable spectacle, where one might see the Goths fighting with lances, the Gepids raging with the sword, the Rugi breaking off the spears in their own wounds, the Suebi fighting on foot, the Huns with bows, the Alans drawing up a battle-line of heavy-armed and the Heruls of light-armed warriors. Finally, after many bitter conflicts, victory fell unexpectedly to the Gepids. For the sword and conspiracy of Ardaric destroyed almost 30,000 men, Huns as well as those of the other nations who brought them aid. (Jordanes)

Fate was no more kind to Aetius than it was to Attila. The emperor Valentinian was never well disposed towards him and with the Hun threat removed his need to rely on Aetius was diminished. On 21 September 454 Valentinian summoned his general to court at Ravenna and killed him with his own hand. The following year Optila and Thraustila, two of Aetius' Hun bodyguards, assassinated Valentinian in turn.

Three years after the battle at the Catalaunian Fields most of the main protagonists were dead. Theodoric died on the field, and his son Thorismund was assassinated by his brother Theodoric II in 453. Attila died that same year and his son Ellac was killed at Nedao in 454. Aetius also met his death in 454. Gaul and Italy were still nominally Roman and the Huns would never again be a threat, but the Western Empire was on her last legs.

In 475 Orestes, Attila's former Roman secretary, made his son Romulus Augustulus emperor with the backing of Herul, Rugian, Scirian and Thuringian mercenaries. Many of them would have been the sons of men who had fought for Attila at the Catalaunian Fields. Under the leadership of Odoacer, these men rose in revolt the following year, killed Orestes and on 4 September 476 deposed Romulus, effectively ending the West Roman Empire forever.

The arms and equipment of these Sarmatian warriors depicted on Trajan's column seem to have become increasingly widespread in latter years of the Roman Empire. Many Romans, Goths, Alans and Huns would have been similarly equipped in the 5th century although horse armour was relatively rare. (Deutsches Archäologisches Institut, Rome)

THE BATTLEFIELD TODAY

There are no monuments, no signposts and no physical reminders of the great battle that took place on the Mauriacian Plains beyond Troyes. Yet the battlefield is well worth a visit.

Troyes itself has an atmospheric medieval centre complete with narrow cobbled streets and ancient timber-frame houses. There are several excellent museums. The Musée Saint-Loup is not to be missed as it contains the treasure of Pouan, which is so far the only archaeological find that may be linked to the battle. In addition to this there is a good collection of Frankish weapons from the 5th–7th centuries alongside Gallo-Roman and Celtic artefacts.

To explore the battlefield itself you will need a car and it helps to have 1:25,000-scale maps from the Institut Géographique National (you will need both maps 2717E and 2817O as – predictably – the battlefield straddles the edges of both). Access to much of the area is along farm lanes that will not be marked on ordinary road maps and satnav is unlikely to be of any help. Driving out from Troyes to the west the dominance of the Montgueux ridge becomes immediately obvious. It stands out in stark contrast to the perfectly flat fields that surround Troyes for many miles around. A single lane track winds its way through vineyards (this is Champagne after all) to the top from where you can see for miles around, just as Thorismund would have in 451.

After surveying the plains from the heights you should head down to the village of Grange-l'Évêque which would have been more or less at the centre of Aetius' line. Then turn south along a farm track towards the foot of the ridge where Thorismund's Visigoths would have ridden down the slope into the flank of the Ostrogoths. Finally it is worth heading north-east across the featureless farm fields to the Seine, following the probable route taken by Attila as he retreated to his camp. This may well have been in the vicinity of Saint-Lyé where there are ruins of an ancient bridge over the river. Looking back from Saint-Lyé towards the Montgueux ridge you can really appreciate the wide-open space and realise why Attila would have chosen this place to do battle.

The medieval centre of Troyes. The Musée Saint-Loup is well worth a visit, especially to see the magnificent treasure of Pouan.

If you have more time it is well worth taking a drive to Sens. There is a modern autoroute which will get you there quickly but on the return to Troyes you should take the D660, which is the old Roman road that Attila would have taken on his retreat from Orléans. Driving along this road, which follows the River Vanne, it is easy to appreciate why the rolling terrain would have not suited Attila's horse archers and why he fell all the way back to Troyes. Sens has a good Gallo-Roman museum but the main attraction is the massive late Roman walls that still stand intact in places, albeit with some later medieval additions. On the way back to Troyes along the D660 it is worth stopping at Fontvannes, the source of the Vanne and the probable place of Aetius' camp the night before the battle. From here you can take the secondary roads up the heights to the north-west until you reach the heights above Grange-l'Évêque. There you can see what Aetius would have seen on the morning of 20 June 451 and ponder the decisions he would have taken.

A drive of 80km north to Châlons-en-Champagne to explore the surrounding area will be enough to convince you that the terrain there does not conform to any of the near contemporary descriptions of the battle, despite the fact that it is commonly known as the Battle of Châlons. From Châlons it is not too far to make a detour to the Musée des Temps Barbares at Marles to the north-west of Reims. Here there is a very good reconstructed Frankish village and an excellent museum devoted to finds from the barbarian invasions of Gaul. The museum frequently hosts re-enactment groups.

BIBLIOGRAPHY AND FURTHER READING

Primary sources

Ammianus Marcelinus, *History*. A 4th-century Roman army officer, Ammianus gives a detailed description of the Huns as they seemed to the Romans when they first burst on the scene in 376. He is also an invaluable source for military activity of the later empire up to the Battle of Adrianople in 378. The full version is available in the Loeb Classical Library and an abridged edition in the Penguin Classics series entitled *The Later Roman Empire: A.D. 354–378*. There is also an online version at http://www.tertullian.org/fathers/ammianus_00_eintro.htm.

Gregory of Tours, *The History of the Franks*, translated by Lewis Thorpe, Penguin Classics (1974). Written by the Gallo-Roman Bishop of Tours in the mid-6th century, this gives a brief account of the battle and the siege of Orléans.

Jordanes, *The Origins and Deeds of the Goths*, translated by Charles C. Mierow and published online by the University of Calgary (http://people.ucalgary.ca/~vandersp/Courses/texts/jordgeti.html). Written around 100 years after the event this is the single most important source on the battle and the armies that fought there.

Notitia Dignitatum. This official listing of all Roman civil and military posts in the early 5th century is an invaluable source on the theoretical organisation of the Roman army at the time as well as providing pictures of shield designs for most units. Several online translations exist with the most detailed modern analysis of the military aspects being Luke Ueda-Sarson's at http://www.ne.jp/asahi/luke/ueda-sarson/NotitiaPatterns.html.

Priscus of Panium. Only fragments of his works remain; however, his famous description of his embassy to Attila still exists. All his surviving fragments are contained in C. D. Gordon (see *Secondary sources*).

Sidonius Apollinaris, *Poems and Letters*, translated by W. B. Anderson, Loeb Classical Library (1936). The surviving letters of this 5th-century Gallo-Roman aristocrat give a fascinating insight into the period. They also provide first-hand accounts of events before and after the battle.

Flavius Vegetius, *De Rei Militari* (*Concerning Military Matters*). Several translations exist including online versions such as http://www.digitalattic.org/home/war/vegetius/. Probably written in the 390s, this military manual describes the training, organisation and tactics of the later Roman army. However, it mixes up historical and contemporary practises with Vegetius' prescription for improvements and should not be taken at face value.

Secondary sources

Bachrach, Bernard S., *A History of the Alans in the West*, University of Minnesota Press (1973). A very useful insight into the Alans, who fought alongside Aetius.

Barker, Phil, *Armies and Enemies of Imperial Rome*, Wargames Research Group (1981). Although primarily written for wargamers and now slightly dated, this book still gives an excellent and easily accessible overview of the later Roman army and its enemies.

Bishop, M. C. and Coulston, Jon C. N., *Roman Military Equipment*, Batsford (1993). An excellent, detailed reference book with a good chapter on late Roman equipment.

Boss, Roy, *Justinian's Wars*, Montvert Publications (1993). Although focused on the 6th century, the author provides interesting and thoughtful insights into the Gothic, Frankish and Roman armies, much of which is applicable to the 5th century.

Bury, Jon B., *The Invasion of Europe by the Barbarians*, Norton Library (1967). A series of lectures by the late Irish historian first published in 1928. Bury gives a good analysis of the events leading up to the battle and clearly identifies Troyes rather than Châlons-en-Champagne as the location. He rejects the idea that the battle was particularly significant.

Delbrück, Hans, *The Barbarian Invasions*, translated by Walter J. Renfroe, University of Nebraska Press (1990). Originally published in German in 1909, this book remains one of the best military studies of the barbarian migrations. Unfortunately Delbrück dismisses the battle with a single sentence saying that there are not enough sources to do it justice.

Drinkwater, John and Elton, Hugh (eds.), *Fifth-century Gaul: A Crisis of Identity*, Cambridge University Press (1990). A collection of academic papers focusing primarily on non-military and non-political subjects. It gives a very good insight into the state of Gaul at the time of Aetius and Attila.

Elton, Hugh, *Warfare in Roman Europe AD 350–425*, The Clarendon Press (1996). An excellent study of the late Roman military system which probably overstates the case for a strong professional Roman army right to the end of empire.

Ferril, Arther, *The Fall of the Roman Empire: The Military Explanation*, Thames & Hudson (1988). This book concludes that Rome's fall was not internal weakness but the deterioration of the Roman army. Some of the conclusions are rather bizarre, such as a faulty analysis which concludes that by 451 the Huns fought on foot.

Fields, Nic, *The Hun: Scourge of God AD 375–565*, Osprey Publishing (2006). This book gives more detail on Hun warriors who fought at Campus Mauriacus.

Gibbon, Sir Edward, *The History of the Decline and Fall of the Roman Empire* (1776–89). This monumental work is still hard to beat despite its age. Originally in six volumes, a number of abridged versions have been published since.

Girard, M. 'Campus Mauriacus: A New Study on the Battlefield of Attila', *Revue Historique* (XXVIII, 1885). The first and only detailed study of the battlefield prior to this Osprey book. M. Girard presents an excellent case for identifying the ridge of Montgueux as the ridge mentioned by Jordanes.

Goldsworthy, Adrian, *The Fall of the West*, Phoenix (2009). A very useful and readable overview written by a military historian although he tends to pass over the Battle of Campus Mauriacus.

Gordon, Colin D., *The Age of Attila*, University of Michigan Press (1966). This incredibly useful book contains the surviving fragments of Priscus, Olympiodorus, Malchus and Joannes Antiochenus.

Halsall, Guy, *Barbarian Migrations and the Roman West, 376–568*, Cambridge Medieval Textbooks (2007). A detailed academic study of the barbarian invasions which integrates archaeological and historical evidence. It is more useful for an insight into the times rather than the battle itself.

Heather, Peter, *The Goths*, Blackwell (1998). An excellent and very readable study of the Goths (both Visi- and Ostro-) although the battle is pretty well glossed over.

Howarth, Patrick, *Attila: King of the Huns*, Constable (1994). An easy to read account of Attila and the Huns.

Jones, Arnold H. M., *The Later Roman Empire, 284–602*, Blackwell (1964). This is probably the most exhaustive study of the later empire, including an exceptionally good chapter on the army and an appendix on the *Notitia Dignitatum*.

——, *The Decline of the Ancient World*, Longman (1966). This is an abridged version of the above book which unfortunately cuts out most of the interesting military bits.

Kelly, Christopher, *Attila the Hun: Barbarian Terror and the Fall of the Roman Empire*, The Bodley Head (2008). A comprehensive account of the Huns, Romans and the events of the 5th century, well written in a non-academic, narrative style.

Lot, Ferdinand, *The End of the Ancient World and the Beginnings of the Middle Ages* (1927). Despite its age this book gives an excellent overview and analysis of the transition from the classical world to early medieval Europe.

MacDowall, Simon, *Late Roman Infantryman AD 236–565*, Osprey Publishing (1994).

——, *Late Roman Cavalryman AD 236–565*. Osprey Publishing (1995).

——, *Germanic Warrior AD 236–568*, Osprey Publishing (1996). These three books in the Osprey Warrior series give more detail on the Romans and Germans who fought at the Catalaunian Fields.

Man, John, *Attila the Hun*, Bantam Books (2005). A highly readable, non-academic book most useful for a chapter detailing the lessons to be learned from Lajos Kassai's revival of mounted archery.

Maenchen-Helfen, Otto J., *The World of the Huns*, University of California Press (1973). This book remains the most complete and detailed study of the Huns.

Moss, J. R. 'The Effects of the Policies of Aetius on the History of Western Europe', *Historia* (LXXII, 1973). An interesting article which concludes that Aetius' fixation on Gaul at the expense of Africa and naval power was fatal to the Western Empire.

Muhlberger, Stephen, *The Fifth-Century Chroniclers: Prosper, Hydatius, and the Gallic Chronicler of 452*, Arca Classical and Medieval Texts (1981). This collection of excerpts from the chronicles gives first-hand accounts of events in the 5th-century West.

Tackholm, Ulf, 'Aetius and the Battle on the Catalaunian Fields', *Opuscula Romana* (VII, 1969). This article is an excellent, detailed analysis of the battle and the events leading up to it.

Thompson, Edward A., *The Huns*, Blackwell Publishing (1999). Although first published in 1949 this book still remains one of the best histories of the Huns and their impact on the Roman Empire. The author also pays more attention to the impact of the Bacaudae than most other historians.

INDEX

Figures in **bold** refer to illustrations.